AF691058

# Web Development Made Simple

## Master HTML, CSS,

## And

## JavaScript to Build Your First Websites

Asher Grey

# Copyright © 2025

All rights reserved. No portion of this book, "Web Development Made Simple: Master HTML, CSS, and JavaScript to Build Your First Websites," may be reproduced, distributed, or transmitted in any form, including digital, print, or electronic formats, without prior written permission from the copyright holder. This includes, but is not limited to, copying, recording, scanning, or sharing online.


First edition, 2025.

# Table of Contents

**Web Development Made Simple: Master HTML, CSS, and JavaScript to Build Your First Websites**

# Chapter 1

# Introduction to Web Development

## 1.1 Why Learn Web Development?

### The Importance of Web Development in the Digital Age

Web development is a cornerstone of the modern digital landscape, serving as the backbone for countless online experiences that define how we interact, work, and communicate. Learning web development is not just about acquiring technical skills; it is about gaining the ability to create, innovate, and contribute to a world increasingly reliant on digital platforms. Websites are the primary interface for businesses, governments, educational institutions, and individuals to share information, sell products, and engage with audiences globally. From e-commerce giants like Amazon to personal blogs, web development enables the creation of these digital spaces, making it a highly valuable and versatile skill.

The demand for skilled web developers continues to grow as businesses and organizations prioritize their online presence. According to industry reports, the global demand for web developers is projected to increase steadily, with job growth in the tech sector outpacing many other industries. This demand is driven by the need for websites that are not only functional but also user-friendly, visually appealing, and optimized for performance across devices. By learning web development, individuals position themselves to tap into this lucrative and dynamic job market, whether as full-time professionals, freelancers, or entrepreneurs building their own platforms.

### Career Opportunities and Flexibility

One of the most compelling reasons to learn web development is the vast array of career opportunities it unlocks. Web developers can specialize in various areas, such as front-end development (focused on user interfaces), back-end development (focused on server-side logic and databases), or full-stack development (encompassing both). Beyond traditional employment, web development skills enable individuals to work as freelancers, offering services to clients worldwide. The rise of remote work has further amplified this flexibility, allowing developers to work from virtually anywhere with an internet connection.

Moreover, web development is a gateway to entrepreneurship. Many successful startups, such as Instagram and Airbnb, were built on the foundation of web technologies. By mastering web development, individuals can create their own websites, applications, or online businesses, turning ideas into reality without needing extensive resources. The ability to prototype and launch digital products quickly makes web development an empowering skill for innovators and creators.

## Creativity and Problem-Solving

Web development is a unique blend of creativity and technical problem-solving. Developers have the opportunity to design visually stunning interfaces, craft seamless user experiences, and solve complex technical challenges. For those with an artistic inclination, front-end development offers a canvas to create engaging designs using tools like HTML, CSS, and JavaScript. For those who enjoy logic and systems thinking, back-end development provides opportunities to build robust systems using languages like Python, Ruby, or Node.js.

This combination of creativity and logic makes web development appealing to a wide range of individuals. Whether designing a responsive layout that adapts to different screen sizes or optimizing a database query for performance, web developers are constantly challenged to think critically and innovate. This dynamic nature ensures that the field remains engaging and intellectually stimulating.

## Accessibility and Low Barrier to Entry

One of the most attractive aspects of web development is its accessibility. Unlike many technical fields that require expensive hardware or specialized education, web development can be learned with minimal resources. A basic computer and an internet connection are often sufficient to start coding. Numerous free or low-cost resources, such as online tutorials, documentation, and open-source tools, are available to aspiring developers. Platforms like freeCodeCamp, Codecademy, and MDN Web Docs provide comprehensive learning paths for beginners.

Furthermore, web development is a field where formal education is not always a prerequisite. Many successful developers are self-taught or have learned through bootcamps and online courses. This low barrier to entry makes web development an inclusive field, accessible to individuals from diverse backgrounds, regardless of their financial situation or prior education.

### Contribution to Society and Innovation

Web development empowers individuals to make a tangible impact on society. Developers can create websites that address social issues, such as platforms for education, healthcare, or environmental awareness. For example, websites like Khan Academy provide free education to millions, while platforms like GoFundMe enable crowdfunding for charitable causes. By learning web development, individuals can contribute to projects that align with their values and drive positive change.

Additionally, web development fuels innovation by enabling the creation of new tools, platforms, and services. The web is a dynamic ecosystem where new technologies, such as progressive web apps (PWAs) and Web3, are constantly emerging. Developers who stay abreast of these trends can lead the charge in shaping the future of the internet, creating solutions that redefine how we interact with technology.

---

## 1.2 Understanding the Web: How Websites Work

### The Architecture of the Web

At its core, the web is a global network of interconnected computers that communicate using standardized protocols to deliver content to users. Understanding how websites work requires grasping the fundamental architecture of the internet, which is built on the client-server model. The client, typically a user's web browser (e.g., Chrome, Firefox, or Safari), sends requests to a server, which hosts the website's files and data. The server processes these requests and returns the requested content, which the browser then renders for the user.

The communication between clients and servers relies on the Hypertext Transfer Protocol (HTTP) or its secure variant, HTTPS. When a user enters a URL (e.g., www.example.com) into their browser, the browser sends an HTTP request to the server hosting the website. The server responds with the necessary files, such as HTML, CSS, and JavaScript, which the browser interprets to display the website. This process, while seemingly instantaneous, involves multiple steps and technologies working in harmony.

## The Role of HTML, CSS, and JavaScript

Websites are primarily built using three core technologies: HTML (Hypertext Markup Language), CSS (Cascading Style Sheets), and JavaScript. These technologies work together to create the structure, style, and interactivity of a website.

- **HTML**: HTML is the backbone of any website, providing its structure and content. It uses a system of tags to define elements like headings, paragraphs, images, and links. For example, a simple HTML document might include a `<header>` for the website's title, a `<nav>` for navigation links, and a `<section>` for the main content. HTML is semantic, meaning it conveys meaning about the content, which is crucial for accessibility and search engine optimization (SEO).

- **CSS**: CSS is responsible for the visual presentation of a website. It controls aspects like colors, fonts, layouts, and responsiveness. For instance, CSS can be used to make a website's layout adapt seamlessly to different screen sizes, ensuring a consistent experience on desktops, tablets, and smartphones. CSS frameworks like Bootstrap and Tailwind CSS simplify the styling process by providing pre-built components and utilities.

- **JavaScript**: JavaScript adds interactivity and dynamic functionality to websites. It enables features like form validation, interactive maps, and real-time updates without requiring a page reload. Modern JavaScript frameworks, such as React, Vue.js, and Angular, allow developers to build complex, single-page applications (SPAs) that behave like desktop or mobile apps.

These three technologies form the foundation of front-end development, which focuses on the user-facing side of a website. However, a fully functional website often involves additional components, such as back-end systems and databases.

## The Client-Server Model and Back-End Development

While the front-end handles what users see and interact with, the back-end manages the server-side logic, data storage, and application functionality. The back-end consists of a server, an application, and a database, often referred to as the "server stack." Popular back-end technologies include Node.js, Python (with frameworks like Django or Flask), Ruby on Rails, and PHP.

When a user interacts with a website, such as submitting a form or making a purchase, the front-end sends a request to the back-end via an API (Application Programming Interface). The back-end processes the request, interacts with the database if necessary, and sends a response back to the front-end. For example, when a user logs into a website, the back-end verifies their credentials against a database and returns a success or failure response.

Databases, such as MySQL, PostgreSQL, or MongoDB, store the website's data, including user profiles, product inventories, or blog posts. The back-end uses server-side languages and frameworks to handle tasks like user authentication, data processing, and content management. This separation of front-end and back-end allows for modular development, where different teams can focus on specific aspects of a website.

## The Role of Web Hosting and Domain Names

For a website to be accessible on the internet, it must be hosted on a server that is always online. Web hosting providers, such as AWS, Google Cloud, or Bluehost, offer servers that store website files and make them available to users worldwide. Hosting services vary in terms of performance, scalability, and cost, with options ranging from shared hosting for small websites to dedicated servers for high-traffic platforms.

Domain names, such as example.com, serve as human-readable addresses for websites. When a user enters a domain name, the browser uses the Domain Name System (DNS) to translate it into an IP address, which identifies the server hosting the website. Registering a domain name and setting up hosting are essential steps in making a website publicly accessible.

## The Importance of Web Standards and Accessibility

The web operates on a set of standards maintained by organizations like the World Wide Web Consortium (W3C). These standards ensure that websites are interoperable across different browsers and devices. For example, adhering to HTML and CSS standards ensures that a website renders consistently whether viewed on Chrome, Firefox, or a mobile browser.

Accessibility is another critical aspect of web development. Websites must be designed to be usable by everyone, including individuals with disabilities. This involves following guidelines like the Web Content Accessibility Guidelines (WCAG), which recommend practices such as providing text alternatives for images, ensuring keyboard navigability, and using sufficient color contrast. Accessible websites not only improve user experience but also expand a website's reach and comply with legal requirements in many regions.

# 1.3 Tools You Need to Get Started

## The Essential Toolkit for Web Development

Embarking on a web development journey requires a set of tools that enable you to write, test, and deploy code efficiently. Fortunately, the barrier to entry is low, as many of these tools are free, open-source, and widely supported by the developer community. Whether you're building a simple static website or a complex web application, having the right tools is crucial for productivity and success. This section explores the essential tools needed to start web development, including text editors, browsers, version control systems, and additional utilities that streamline the development process.

### Text Editors and Integrated Development Environments (IDEs)

A text editor or IDE is the primary tool for writing code. While a basic text editor like Notepad (Windows) or TextEdit (macOS) can technically be used, specialized tools offer features like syntax highlighting, autocompletion, and debugging, which significantly enhance productivity.

- **Visual Studio Code (VS Code)**: VS Code, developed by Microsoft, is one of the most popular text editors among web developers. It's lightweight, highly customizable, and supports a vast ecosystem of extensions for languages like HTML, CSS, JavaScript, and more. Features like integrated Git support, a built-in terminal, and IntelliSense (code autocompletion) make it ideal for beginners and professionals alike.
- **Sublime Text**: Known for its speed and simplicity, Sublime Text is another excellent choice. It offers powerful features like multiple cursors and a distraction-free mode, making it great for quick edits and focused coding sessions.
- **Atom**: Developed by GitHub, Atom is an open-source editor with a similar feel to VS Code. It's highly customizable and supports plugins for enhanced functionality, though it's slightly heavier in terms of resource usage.
- **JetBrains WebStorm**: For developers seeking a full-fledged IDE, WebStorm provides advanced features like intelligent code refactoring, debugging, and

support for frameworks like React and Angular. However, it's a paid tool, though a free trial is available.

For beginners, VS Code is recommended due to its balance of simplicity, performance, and community support. Extensions like Prettier (for code formatting) and Live Server (for real-time previewing of web pages) can further enhance the development experience.

### Web Browsers and Developer Tools

Web browsers are essential for testing and debugging websites. Modern browsers like Google Chrome, Mozilla Firefox, Microsoft Edge, and Safari come with built-in developer tools that allow you to inspect HTML elements, debug JavaScript, and analyze performance.

- **Google Chrome**: Chrome's DevTools are widely regarded as the gold standard for web development. They offer features like the Elements panel for inspecting and editing HTML/CSS, the Console for debugging JavaScript, and the Network panel for monitoring resource loading times.
- **Mozilla Firefox**: Firefox's Developer Edition provides advanced tools tailored for web developers, including a powerful CSS Grid inspector and enhanced JavaScript debugging capabilities.
- **Safari and Edge**: While Chrome and Firefox dominate, testing on Safari (for Apple devices) and Edge ensures cross-browser compatibility, which is critical for delivering a consistent user experience.

Browsers also support extensions like Web Developer Toolbar and ColorZilla, which provide additional utilities for tasks like inspecting CSS properties or picking colors from web pages.

### Version Control Systems

Version control is essential for managing code changes, collaborating with others, and maintaining project history. Git, a distributed version control system, is the industry standard for web development.

- **Git**: Git allows developers to track changes, create branches for experimenting with features, and revert to previous versions if needed. It's typically used with platforms like GitHub, GitLab, or Bitbucket for hosting repositories and enabling collaboration.

- **GitHub Desktop**: For beginners, GitHub Desktop provides a user-friendly interface for managing Git repositories without needing to use command-line commands.
- **Command-Line Tools**: Learning basic Git commands (e.g., `git init`, `git commit`, `git push`) is highly recommended, as they provide greater control and are widely used in professional settings.

Version control is particularly valuable for team projects, as it allows multiple developers to work on the same codebase without conflicts.

### Package Managers and Build Tools

Modern web development often involves managing dependencies and automating repetitive tasks. Package managers and build tools streamline these processes.

- **npm and Yarn**: npm (Node Package Manager) and Yarn are used to install and manage JavaScript libraries and frameworks, such as React or Bootstrap. They simplify the process of adding third-party code to your projects.
- **Webpack and Vite**: These build tools bundle and optimize assets like JavaScript, CSS, and images. Vite, in particular, is gaining popularity for its speed and simplicity in modern JavaScript projects.
- **Task Runners**: Tools like Gulp or npm scripts automate tasks such as minifying CSS, compiling Sass, or refreshing the browser during development.

For beginners, starting with npm and a simple setup (e.g., using Live Server for real-time previews) is sufficient, with more advanced tools introduced as projects grow in complexity.

### Additional Utilities

Several other tools can enhance the development workflow:

- **CodePen or JSFiddle**: These online code editors allow you to experiment with HTML, CSS, and JavaScript in real time, making them great for prototyping and sharing code snippets.
- **Postman**: For developers working with APIs, Postman is a tool for testing and debugging API requests.

- **Figma or Adobe XD**: While not strictly development tools, these design tools are useful for creating wireframes and mockups, especially for front-end developers focused on UI/UX.
- **Command-Line Interface (CLI)**: Familiarity with the terminal (e.g., Bash, PowerShell, or Zsh) is valuable for tasks like installing dependencies, running servers, or managing Git.

---

# 1.4 Setting Up Your Development Environment

## The Foundation of Efficient Web Development

Setting up a development environment is a critical step in your web development journey. A well-configured environment ensures that you can write, test, and debug code efficiently while minimizing setup-related frustrations. This section provides a comprehensive guide to setting up a development environment, covering operating system considerations, software installation, configuration of tools, and best practices for maintaining an organized workspace.

### Choosing an Operating System

Web development is platform-agnostic, meaning you can work on Windows, macOS, or Linux. Each operating system has its advantages:

- **Windows**: Widely used and beginner-friendly, Windows supports all major development tools. Tools like Windows Subsystem for Linux (WSL) allow you to run a Linux environment within Windows, providing access to Unix-like tools.
- **macOS**: Popular among developers for its Unix-based architecture and seamless integration with tools like Homebrew (a package manager). macOS is particularly favored for front-end development due to its design-focused ecosystem.
- **Linux**: Preferred by many back-end developers for its open-source nature and compatibility with server environments. Distributions like Ubuntu or Fedora are lightweight and customizable, making them ideal for development.

For beginners, Windows or macOS is recommended due to their user-friendly interfaces, but Linux is a great choice for those comfortable with command-line workflows.

### Installing a Text Editor

The first step in setting up your environment is installing a text editor or IDE. Visual Studio Code (VS Code) is a versatile choice due to its extensive feature set and community support. To install VS Code:

1. Visit the official VS Code website (code.visualstudio.com) and download the installer for your operating system.
2. Run the installer and follow the prompts to complete the installation.
3. Open VS Code and install essential extensions, such as:
    - **Prettier**: For automatic code formatting.
    - **Live Server**: For real-time previewing of HTML/CSS/JavaScript.
    - **ESLint**: For JavaScript linting and error detection.
    - **HTML CSS Support**: For enhanced HTML/CSS autocompletion.

Configure VS Code settings (e.g., font size, theme, or auto-save) to suit your preferences by accessing the settings menu (File > Preferences > Settings).

### Setting Up Version Control with Git

Git is essential for managing code and collaborating with others. To set up Git:

1. Download and install Git from git-scm.com.

Configure Git with your name and email:
git config --global user.name "Your Name"

git config --global user.email "your.email@example.com"

2.
3. Create a GitHub account (github.com) and set up a repository for your projects.
4. Optionally, install GitHub Desktop for a graphical interface, or learn basic Git commands like `git clone`, `git add`, `git commit`, and `git push`.

To integrate Git with VS Code, install the Git extension and connect it to your GitHub account for seamless version control.

### Installing Node.js and npm

Node.js is a runtime environment that allows you to run JavaScript outside the browser, while npm (Node Package Manager) manages dependencies. To install:

1. Download the latest LTS (Long-Term Support) version of Node.js from nodejs.org.
2. Run the installer, which automatically includes npm.

Verify the installation by running:
node --version

npm --version

3.

Use npm to install global packages, such as:
npm install -g live-server

4. This installs Live Server, which allows you to preview web pages locally with automatic reloading.

**Configuring a Local Development Server**

A local development server is useful for testing websites before deployment. Tools like Live Server (a VS Code extension) or http-server (an npm package) create a local server for previewing your work. To set up http-server:

Install it globally:
npm install -g http-server

1.

Navigate to your project folder in the terminal:
cd path/to/your/project

2.

Start the server:
http-server

3.
4. Open your browser and visit `http://localhost:8080` to view your website.

For more complex projects, frameworks like Vite or Create React App provide built-in development servers with advanced features.

### Organizing Your Workspace

An organized workspace improves efficiency. Create a dedicated folder for your projects (e.g., `C:\Dev\Projects` on Windows or `~/Projects` on macOS/Linux). Within each project, use a consistent structure, such as:

```
project-name/
├── css/
├── js/
├── images/
├── index.html
```

Back up your work regularly using cloud storage (e.g., Google Drive, Dropbox) or GitHub repositories. Keep your tools and dependencies updated to avoid compatibility issues.

### Testing and Debugging Setup

Ensure your browser's developer tools are accessible (usually via F12 or right-click > Inspect). Test your code across multiple browsers to ensure compatibility. For JavaScript debugging, use VS Code's built-in debugger or Chrome DevTools' Sources panel. Install extensions like ESLint to catch errors early.

---

# 1.5 Your First Web Page: A Sneak Peek

## Building Your First Website

Creating your first web page is an exciting milestone in your web development journey. It introduces you to the core technologies—HTML, CSS, and JavaScript—and provides a hands-on opportunity to see how they work together. This section guides you through building a simple, functional web page, explaining each step in detail and providing a foundation for further learning. By the end, you'll have a basic webpage that displays text, images, and interactive elements.

### Understanding the Goal

The goal is to create a simple personal portfolio page that includes a heading, a brief introduction, an image, and a button that triggers a JavaScript action. This project will demonstrate the roles of HTML (structure), CSS (styling), and JavaScript (interactivity) while keeping the scope manageable for beginners.

### Step 1: Setting Up the Project

Create a new folder for your project, named `portfolio`. Inside it, create three files:

- `index.html`: The main HTML file.
- `styles.css`: The CSS file for styling.
- `script.js`: The JavaScript file for interactivity.

You can create these files using VS Code or any text editor. Ensure your development environment (set up as described in Section 1.4) includes a local server like Live Server for real-time previews.

### Step 2: Writing the HTML

HTML provides the structure of your webpage. In `index.html`, add the following code:

```
<!DOCTYPE html>

<html lang="en">

<head>

  <meta charset="UTF-8">

  <meta name="viewport" content="width=device-width, initial-scale=1.0">

  <title>My First Portfolio</title>

  <link rel="stylesheet" href="styles.css">

</head>

<body>
```

```
  <header>
    <h1>Welcome to My Portfolio</h1>
  </header>
  <main>
    <section>
      <h2>About Me</h2>
      <p>Hi, I'm learning web development! This is my first webpage, built with
HTML, CSS, and JavaScript.</p>
      <img src="https://via.placeholder.com/300" alt="Placeholder image">
      <button onclick="showMessage()">Click Me!</button>
    </section>
  </main>
  <script src="script.js"></script>
</body>
</html>
```

This HTML includes:

- A `<!DOCTYPE html>` declaration to specify the document type.
- A `<head>` section with metadata (charset, viewport) and a link to the CSS file.
- A `<body>` containing a header, a main section with text, an image (using a placeholder URL), and a button linked to a JavaScript function.
- A `<script>` tag to include the JavaScript file.

**Step 3: Styling with CSS**

CSS makes your webpage visually appealing. In `styles.css`, add:

```
body {
   font-family: Arial, sans-serif;
   margin: 0;
   padding: 20px;
   background-color: #f4f4f4;
}

header {
   text-align: center;
   background-color: #333;
   color: white;
   padding: 10px;
}

h1, h2 {
   color: #333;
}

section {
   max-width: 600px;
   margin: 20px auto;
```

```
    padding: 20px;

    background-color: white;

    border-radius: 8px;

    box-shadow: 0 0 10px rgba(0, 0, 0, 0.1);

}


img {

    display: block;

    margin: 20px auto;

    max-width: 100%;

}


button {

    display: block;

    margin: 20px auto;

    padding: 10px 20px;

    background-color: #333;

    color: white;

    border: none;

    border-radius: 5px;

    cursor: pointer;

}
```

```
button:hover {
    background-color: #555;
}
```

This CSS:

- Sets a clean, modern font and background color for the body.
- Styles the header with a dark background and white text.
- Centers and styles the main content section with a card-like appearance.
- Ensures the image is responsive and centered.
- Styles the button with a hover effect for interactivity.

**Step 4: Adding Interactivity with JavaScript**

JavaScript adds dynamic behavior. In `script.js`, add:

```
function showMessage() {
    alert("Welcome to my portfolio! I'm excited to learn web development!");
}
```

This simple function displays a pop-up alert when the button is clicked. The `onclick="showMessage()"` attribute in the HTML links the button to this function.

**Step 5: Testing Your Webpage**

To view your webpage:

1. Open `index.html` in VS Code.
2. Right-click and select "Open with Live Server" (if using the Live Server extension) or open the file in a browser via `http://localhost:8080` (if using http-server).
3. Verify that:

    - The heading and text display correctly.
    - The image loads and is centered.
    - The button triggers the alert when clicked.
    - The styling (colors, layout, hover effect) matches the CSS.

If issues arise, use Chrome DevTools (F12) to inspect elements or check the Console for JavaScript errors.

**Step 6: Next Steps and Enhancements**

Your first webpage is a starting point. To enhance it, consider:

- Adding more sections (e.g., a portfolio gallery or contact form).
- Using CSS frameworks like Bootstrap for advanced styling.
- Incorporating more JavaScript, such as dynamic content updates or form validation.
- Deploying the webpage to a hosting service like GitHub Pages or Netlify.

# Chapter 2

# HTML – Building the Skeleton of Your Website

## 2.1 What is HTML? The Foundation of Web Pages

### The Role of HTML in Web Development

HTML, or Hypertext Markup Language, is the cornerstone of web development, serving as the foundational language for creating and structuring content on the World Wide Web. It provides the essential framework that defines the structure and content of a webpage, acting as the skeleton upon which all other web technologies, such as CSS for styling and JavaScript for interactivity, are built. Without HTML, websites would lack the basic structure needed to display text, images, links, and other elements in a browser. As the primary markup language used by developers, HTML is indispensable for anyone looking to create websites or web applications, making it the first skill to master for aspiring web developers.

HTML was first introduced by Tim Berners-Lee in 1990 as part of the creation of the World Wide Web. Since then, it has evolved through multiple versions, with HTML5 being the current standard as of 2025. HTML5 introduced powerful features like semantic elements, multimedia support, and APIs for enhanced interactivity, solidifying HTML's role as a versatile and essential tool in modern web development. Its simplicity and universality make it accessible to beginners while providing robust capabilities for advanced developers building complex applications.

### How HTML Works

At its core, HTML is a markup language, meaning it uses a system of tags to annotate and organize content. These tags tell web browsers how to interpret and display the content, whether it's a heading, paragraph, image, or link. When a user visits a website, their browser downloads the HTML file from a server, parses its structure, and renders the content visually. This process is seamless to the user but relies on HTML's ability to define the hierarchy and relationships between different elements on the page.

For example, an HTML document might include a `<h1>` tag for a main heading, a `<p>` tag for a paragraph, and an `<img>` tag for an image. These tags are enclosed in angle brackets, and most come in pairs (an opening tag and a closing tag) to wrap the content they describe. The browser interprets these tags to create a visual layout, ensuring that headings are larger, paragraphs are formatted as blocks of text, and images are displayed correctly.

## The Importance of HTML in the Web Ecosystem

HTML is the backbone of the web because it provides a standardized way to structure content that is universally understood by browsers across different devices and platforms. This standardization, maintained by the World Wide Web Consortium (W3C), ensures that websites function consistently whether viewed on Chrome, Firefox, Safari, or mobile browsers. HTML's role extends beyond static content; it integrates with CSS to control appearance and JavaScript to add interactivity, forming the trifecta of front-end web development.

Moreover, HTML is critical for accessibility and search engine optimization (SEO). Properly structured HTML makes websites accessible to screen readers and assistive technologies, ensuring that users with disabilities can navigate and understand the content. For SEO, search engines like Google rely on HTML tags to index and rank webpages, making clean and semantic HTML essential for visibility in search results.

## HTML5: The Modern Standard

HTML5, released in 2014, revolutionized web development by introducing features that reduced reliance on external plugins like Flash. Key advancements include:

- **Semantic Elements**: Tags like `<header>`, `<footer>`, `<article>`, and `<section>` improve the clarity and structure of HTML, making it easier for developers and browsers to understand the purpose of different sections.
- **Multimedia Support**: Tags like `<video>` and `<audio>` allow native embedding of media without third-party plugins.

- **Canvas and SVG**: HTML5 introduced the `<canvas>` element for dynamic graphics and Scalable Vector Graphics (SVG) for high-quality, scalable visuals.
- **APIs**: HTML5 includes APIs for geolocation, drag-and-drop, and offline storage, enabling developers to build sophisticated web applications.

These features make HTML5 not only a markup language but also a platform for creating rich, interactive experiences, such as games, dashboards, and progressive web apps (PWAs).

## Why Learn HTML?

Learning HTML is essential for several reasons:

- **Foundation for Web Development**: HTML is the starting point for building any website or web application. Without it, there's no structure for CSS or JavaScript to enhance.
- **Low Barrier to Entry**: HTML is beginner-friendly, requiring only a text editor and a browser to get started. Its straightforward syntax allows newcomers to see results quickly.
- **Versatility**: HTML is used in virtually every web-related project, from simple blogs to complex e-commerce platforms.
- **Career Opportunities**: Proficiency in HTML is a prerequisite for web development roles, whether front-end, back-end, or full-stack.
- **Creative Expression**: HTML enables developers to create digital content that reaches a global audience, combining technical precision with creative design.

## Getting Started with HTML

To begin working with HTML, you need minimal tools: a text editor (e.g., Visual Studio Code) and a web browser. Create a file with a `.html` extension, write your code, and open it in a browser to see the results. Online platforms like CodePen or JSFiddle also allow you to experiment with HTML in real-time. As you progress, you'll combine HTML with CSS and JavaScript to build fully functional websites.

---

# 2.2 HTML Elements, Tags, and Attributes

## Understanding HTML Elements

HTML elements are the building blocks of a webpage, defining its structure and content. An element typically consists of a start tag, content, and an end tag, though some elements are self-closing. For example, a paragraph element is written as `<p>This is a paragraph.</p>`, where `<p>` is the start tag, `This is a paragraph.` is the content, and `</p>` is the end tag. Elements can be nested to create complex structures, such as a `<div>` containing multiple `<p>` or `<img>` elements.

Each element serves a specific purpose, from defining headings (`<h1>` to `<h6>`) to embedding images (`<img>`) or creating links (`<a>`). The combination of elements forms a tree-like structure called the Document Object Model (DOM), which browsers use to render the page and which JavaScript can manipulate for dynamic effects.

## Tags: The Syntax of HTML

Tags are the core components of HTML elements, written inside angle brackets (`<` and `>`). Most tags come in pairs:

- **Start Tag**: Indicates the beginning of an element (e.g., `<div>`).
- **End Tag**: Indicates the end, with a forward slash (e.g., `</div>`).
- **Content**: The text or other elements between the start and end tags.

Some tags are self-closing, meaning they don't require an end tag. For example, the image tag `<img src="image.jpg" alt="Description">` is self-closing because it doesn't contain nested content. Other self-closing tags include `<br>` (line break) and `<hr>` (horizontal rule).

Tags must follow specific rules:

- Tags are case-insensitive, but lowercase is the convention in modern HTML (e.g., `<div>` instead of `<DIV>`).
- Tags must be properly nested. For example, `<div><p>Text</p></div>` is correct, while `<div><p>Text</div></p>` is invalid.

- HTML documents must start with a `<!DOCTYPE html>` declaration to specify the HTML version (HTML5 in this case).

## Attributes: Enhancing Elements

Attributes provide additional information about an element, modifying its behavior or appearance. They are included in the start tag and follow the format `name="value"`. For example:

<a href="https://example.com">Visit Example</a>

Here, `href` is the attribute name, and `https://example.com` is its value, specifying the link's destination.

Common attributes include:

- **id**: Uniquely identifies an element (e.g., `<div id="main">`). Used for CSS styling or JavaScript manipulation.
- **class**: Assigns one or more classes for styling or scripting (e.g., `<p class="intro">`).
- **src**: Specifies the source file for media, like images or videos (e.g., `<img src="photo.jpg">`).
- **alt**: Provides alternative text for accessibility (e.g., `<img alt="Description">`).
- **href**: Defines the URL for links (e.g., `<a href="page.html">`).
- **style**: Applies inline CSS (e.g., `<p style="color: blue;">`).

Attributes are critical for functionality, accessibility, and styling. For instance, the `alt` attribute ensures that screen readers can describe images to visually impaired users, while the `id` and `class` attributes enable targeted styling and scripting.

## Common HTML Elements

HTML offers a wide range of elements, categorized by their purpose:

- **Structural Elements**: `<div>`, `<section>`, `<article>`, `<header>`, `<footer>` organize content.

- **Text Elements**: `<h1>` to `<h6>` (headings), `<p>` (paragraphs), `<strong>` (bold), `<em>` (italic) format text.
- **Media Elements**: `<img>`, `<video>`, `<audio>` embed multimedia.
- **Interactive Elements**: `<a>` (links), `<button>`, `<form>`, `<input>` enable user interaction.
- **Metadata Elements**: `<meta>`, `<title>`, `<link>` define document properties in the `<head>`.

For example, a simple webpage might include:

```
<!DOCTYPE html>

<html lang="en">

<head>

  <meta charset="UTF-8">

  <title>My Page</title>

</head>

<body>

  <h1>Welcome</h1>

  <p>This is a <strong>sample</strong> page.</p>

  <a href="about.html">Learn More</a>

  <img src="image.jpg" alt="Sample image">

</body>

</html>
```

## Best Practices for Tags and Attributes

To write clean and maintainable HTML:

- Use lowercase tags for consistency.
- Always close paired tags and include required attributes (e.g., `alt` for `<img>`).
- Avoid inline styles (e.g., `<p style="color: blue;">`) in favor of external CSS files.
- Validate your HTML using tools like the W3C Markup Validator to catch errors.
- Use meaningful attribute values, such as descriptive `id` and `class` names (e.g., `class="main-content"` instead of `class="div1"`).

### The Power of Attributes in Dynamic Webpages

Attributes play a key role in dynamic webpages. For example, the `data-*` attributes (e.g., `data-user-id="123"`) allow developers to store custom data, which JavaScript can access to create interactive features. Similarly, attributes like `aria-*` (e.g., `aria-label`) enhance accessibility by providing additional context for assistive technologies.

---

## 2.3 Structuring Content with Semantic HTML

### What is Semantic HTML?

Semantic HTML refers to the use of HTML elements that convey meaning about the content they contain, rather than just defining its appearance. Unlike non-semantic elements like `<div>` or `<span>`, which are generic containers, semantic elements like `<header>`, `<nav>`, `<article>`, and `<footer>` describe their purpose, making the code more readable, accessible, and SEO-friendly. Semantic HTML, introduced prominently in HTML5, is a best practice for modern web development, as it enhances the clarity and functionality of webpages.

For example, a `<nav>` element clearly indicates a navigation menu, while an `<article>` element denotes a self-contained piece of content, such as a blog post. This semantic structure helps browsers, search engines, and assistive technologies understand the page's organization, improving user experience and discoverability.

## Benefits of Semantic HTML

Using semantic HTML offers several advantages:

- **Improved Accessibility**: Screen readers and assistive technologies rely on semantic elements to interpret content for users with disabilities. For example, a `<nav>` element signals a navigation section, allowing users to jump to it easily.
- **Better SEO**: Search engines prioritize semantic HTML because it provides context about the content. A page with a clear `<h1>` heading and structured `<article>` elements is more likely to rank higher.
- **Easier Maintenance**: Semantic code is self-documenting, making it easier for developers to understand and maintain. For instance, `<footer>` is more intuitive than `<div class="bottom">`.
- **Enhanced Browser Support**: Semantic elements are designed to work seamlessly with modern browsers, ensuring consistent rendering and compatibility.

## Key Semantic Elements in HTML5

HTML5 introduced a range of semantic elements to replace generic containers like `<div>`. Common semantic elements include:

- `<header>`: Represents introductory content, such as a logo or site title.
- `<nav>`: Defines a navigation menu with links to other pages or sections.
- `<main>`: Contains the primary content of the page, unique to each document.
- `<article>`: Represents independent, self-contained content, like a blog post or news article.
- `<section>`: Groups related content, often with a heading.
- `<aside>`: Contains secondary content, such as sidebars or callouts.
- `<footer>`: Holds footer content, like copyright information or contact details.
- `<figure>` **and** `<figcaption>`: Used for images or diagrams with captions.

For example:

<!DOCTYPE html>

<html lang="en">

```html
<head>
    <meta charset="UTF-8">
    <title>Semantic Example</title>
</head>
<body>
    <header>
        <h1>My Blog</h1>
        <nav>
            <ul>
                <li><a href="home.html">Home</a></li>
                <li><a href="about.html">About</a></li>
            </ul>
        </nav>
    </header>
    <main>
        <article>
            <h2>Post Title</h2>
            <p>This is a blog post.</p>
        </article>
    </main>
    <footer>
        <p>&copy; 2025 My Blog</p>
```

```
    </footer>

</body>

</html>
```

This structure clearly defines the page's layout, making it intuitive for developers and machines alike.

## Semantic vs. Non-Semantic HTML

Non-semantic elements like <div> and <span> are still widely used but lack inherent meaning. For example, <div class="header"> can function as a header, but it requires additional context (via classes or IDs) to convey its purpose. In contrast, <header> is self-explanatory. While <div> is versatile for styling and layout, overusing it can lead to "div soup," where the code becomes cluttered and hard to maintain. Semantic HTML reduces reliance on non-semantic elements, improving clarity and reducing code complexity.

## Best Practices for Semantic HTML

To maximize the benefits of semantic HTML:

- Use semantic elements where appropriate (e.g., <nav> for menus, not <div class="menu">).
- Ensure each page has one <main> element for the primary content.
- Use headings (<h1> to <h6>) in a logical hierarchy to outline content.
- Include accessibility attributes, such as aria-label or role, to enhance semantic meaning (e.g., <nav role="navigation">).
- Avoid using semantic elements for styling purposes (e.g., don't use <h1> just to make text larger; use CSS instead).
- Validate your HTML with tools like the W3C Markup Validator to ensure semantic correctness.

### Semantic HTML and Accessibility

Semantic HTML is a cornerstone of web accessibility. Assistive technologies rely on semantic elements to navigate and interpret content. For example, a screen reader can use `<nav>` to allow users to skip to navigation links or `<main>` to focus on the primary content. Attributes like `aria-label`, `aria-hidden`, and `role` further enhance accessibility by providing additional context. For instance:

```
<button aria-label="Close menu">X</button>
```

This ensures that screen readers announce the button's purpose clearly.

### Semantic HTML in Modern Web Development

In modern web development, semantic HTML integrates seamlessly with frameworks like React or Vue.js. For example, React components can map to semantic elements, ensuring that dynamic applications maintain a clear structure. Additionally, semantic HTML supports progressive enhancement, allowing basic content to remain accessible even if JavaScript or CSS fails to load.

## 2.4 Creating Links and Navigation

### The Importance of Links in Web Development

Links, or hyperlinks, are a fundamental feature of the web, enabling navigation between pages, resources, and external websites. They transform the internet into a connected network, allowing users to move seamlessly from one piece of content to another. In HTML, links are created using the `<a>` (anchor) element, which is versatile and essential for building intuitive navigation systems. Effective navigation enhances user experience by providing clear pathways to explore a website's content, making it a critical skill for web developers. This section explores how to create links, structure navigation menus, and implement best practices for usability and accessibility.

### The `<a>` Element and Hyperlinks

The `<a>` element is used to create hyperlinks, with the `href` attribute specifying the destination. The basic syntax is:

```
<a href="https://example.com">Visit Example</a>
```

Here, `href` (hypertext reference) defines the URL, and the text between the opening and closing tags (e.g., "Visit Example") is the clickable link text. The `href` attribute can point to:

- **External URLs**: Links to other websites (e.g., `href="https://google.com"`).
- **Internal Pages**: Links to other pages within the same website (e.g., `href="about.html"`).
- **Page Sections**: Links to specific sections within a page using an ID (e.g., `href="#section1"`).
- **Other Resources**: Files like PDFs or email addresses (e.g., `href="mailto:info@example.com"`).

For example:

```
<a href="contact.html">Contact Us</a>

<a href="#footer">Go to Footer</a>

<a href="mailto:support@example.com">Email Support</a>
```

## Internal vs. External Links

- **Internal Links**: Connect pages within the same website. Use relative paths (e.g., `href="blog/post1.html"`) for simplicity, assuming the file is in a subdirectory. Relative paths are portable and don't require the full domain.

**External Links**: Point to external websites. Use absolute URLs (e.g., `href="https://example.com"`). For external links, it's a good practice to include the `target="_blank"` attribute to open the link in a new tab, improving user

experience:
<a href="https://example.com" target="_blank" rel="noopener">Visit Example</a>

- The `rel="noopener"` attribute enhances security by preventing the new tab from accessing the original page's context.

## Creating Navigation Menus

A navigation menu, typically placed in a `<nav>` element, organizes links to guide users through a website. A common approach is to use an unordered list (`<ul>`) for the menu items:

```
<nav>

  <ul>

    <li><a href="index.html">Home</a></li>

    <li><a href="about.html">About</a></li>

    <li><a href="services.html">Services</a></li>

    <li><a href="contact.html">Contact</a></li>

  </ul>

</nav>
```

This structure is semantic, accessible, and easy to style with CSS. For example, CSS can transform the list into a horizontal menu:

```
nav ul {

  list-style: none;

  display: flex;

  gap: 20px;

}
```

```
nav a {
    text-decoration: none;
    color: #333;
}
nav a:hover {
    color: #007bff;
}
```

## Anchor Links for In-Page Navigation

Anchor links allow users to jump to specific sections within a page. Assign an `id` attribute to the target element, and use a hash (`#`) in the `href`:

```
<a href="#section1">Go to Section 1</a>
<section id="section1">
    <h2>Section 1</h2>
    <p>Content here...</p>
</section>
```

Smooth scrolling can be added with CSS:

```
html {
    scroll-behavior: smooth;
}
```

## Accessibility and Best Practices

To ensure links and navigation are user-friendly and accessible:

- **Descriptive Link Text**: Use meaningful text (e.g., "Read Our Blog" instead of "Click Here") to inform users of the link's purpose, especially for screen readers.

**ARIA Attributes**: Enhance accessibility with attributes like `aria-current="page"` to indicate the active page in a navigation menu:

```
<li><a href="index.html" aria-current="page">Home</a></li>
```

-

**Keyboard Navigation**: Ensure links are focusable using the `Tab` key. Avoid removing the default focus outline unless replaced with a custom style:

```
a:focus {

  outline: 2px solid #007bff;

}
```

-
- **Consistent Navigation**: Place navigation menus in predictable locations (e.g., top or sidebar) and maintain consistency across pages.
- **Test Across Devices**: Ensure navigation is usable on mobile devices, possibly using a hamburger menu for smaller screens.

## Advanced Navigation Techniques

For larger websites, advanced navigation patterns include:

- **Mega Menus**: Dropdown menus with rich content, styled with CSS or JavaScript.
- **Sticky Navigation**: A `<nav>` that remains fixed at the top using `position: sticky` in CSS.
- **Responsive Navigation**: Menus that adapt to screen size, often toggled with JavaScript on mobile devices.

For example, a responsive navigation toggle:

```
<nav>
  <button onclick="toggleMenu()">Menu</button>
  <ul id="menu" class="hidden">
    <li><a href="index.html">Home</a></li>
    <li><a href="about.html">About</a></li>
  </ul>
</nav>
<script>
  function toggleMenu() {
    document.getElementById('menu').classList.toggle('hidden');
  }
</script>
<style>
  .hidden {
    display: none;
  }
  @media (min-width: 768px) {
    .hidden {
      display: flex;
    }
    button {
      display: none;
```

```
    }

  }

</style>
```

# 2.5 Embedding Images and Multimedia

## The Role of Multimedia in Web Development

Multimedia elements, such as images, videos, and audio, are essential for creating engaging and dynamic websites. They enhance user experience by adding visual appeal, conveying information, and supporting interactive features. HTML provides dedicated elements like <img>, <video>, and <audio> to embed multimedia, with HTML5 introducing native support that eliminates the need for external plugins like Flash. This section covers how to embed images and multimedia, optimize them for performance and accessibility, and follow best practices for modern web development.

## Embedding Images with <img>

The <img> element is used to embed images, with two key attributes:

- **src**: Specifies the image file's path or URL (e.g., src="photo.jpg" or src="https://example.com/image.jpg").
- **alt**: Provides alternative text for accessibility and SEO (e.g., alt="Sunset over mountains").

Example:

```
<img src="images/sunset.jpg" alt="A colorful sunset over the mountains">
```

The alt attribute is crucial for:

- **Accessibility**: Screen readers describe the image to visually impaired users.
- **SEO**: Search engines use `alt` text to index images.
- **Fallback**: If the image fails to load, the `alt` text is displayed.

Additional attributes include:

- **width** and **height**: Set the image's dimensions (e.g., `width="300" height="200"`) to prevent layout shifts during loading.
- **title**: Provides a tooltip on hover (e.g., `title="Click to enlarge"`).
- **loading**: Controls loading behavior (e.g., `loading="lazy"` for images below the fold to improve performance).

For responsive images, use the `<picture>` element or `srcset` attribute:

```
<picture>

  <source media="(max-width: 600px)" srcset="small-image.jpg">

  <source media="(min-width: 601px)" srcset="large-image.jpg">

  <img src="fallback-image.jpg" alt="Responsive image">

</picture>
```

This delivers the appropriate image based on screen size, optimizing performance.

## Embedding Videos with `<video>`

The `<video>` element embeds video content natively. Key attributes include:

- **src**: Specifies the video file (e.g., `src="video.mp4"`).
- **controls**: Adds playback controls (e.g., play, pause, volume).
- **poster**: Displays an image before the video plays (e.g., `poster="thumbnail.jpg"`).

Example:

```
<video src="video.mp4" controls poster="thumbnail.jpg" width="600">
```

```
    Your browser does not support the video tag.

</video>
```

The text between the tags serves as fallback content for unsupported browsers. To support multiple formats (e.g., MP4, WebM), use <source>:

```
<video controls width="600">

    <source src="video.mp4" type="video/mp4">

    <source src="video.webm" type="video/webm">

    Your browser does not support the video tag.

</video>
```

Additional attributes like autoplay, loop, and muted control behavior, but use them sparingly to avoid annoying users (e.g., autoplay requires muted for most browsers).

## Embedding Audio with <audio>

The <audio> element embeds audio files, with similar attributes to <video>:

```
<audio src="audio.mp3" controls>

    Your browser does not support the audio tag.

</audio>
```

Multiple formats can be specified:

```
<audio controls>

    <source src="audio.mp3" type="audio/mpeg">
```

```
    <source src="audio.ogg" type="audio/ogg">

    Your browser does not support the audio tag.

</audio>
```

Attributes like `loop` and `autoplay` are available, but `autoplay` should be used cautiously.

## Optimizing Multimedia for Performance

Multimedia files can significantly impact page load times. Optimization strategies include:

- **Compression**: Use tools like TinyPNG for images or HandBrake for videos to reduce file sizes without sacrificing quality.
- **Modern Formats**: Use WebP or AVIF for images and WebM for videos for better compression and quality.
- **Lazy Loading**: Apply `loading="lazy"` to images and videos below the fold.
- **Content Delivery Networks (CDNs)**: Host media on CDNs to improve load times globally.
- **Responsive Images**: Use `srcset` or <picture> to serve appropriately sized images.

## Accessibility Considerations

To make multimedia accessible:

- Always provide descriptive `alt` text for images.

Include captions or transcripts for videos and audio using <track>:

```
<video controls>

    <source src="video.mp4" type="video/mp4">

    <track src="captions.vtt" kind="subtitles" srclang="en" label="English">

</video>
```

- 
- Ensure media controls are keyboard-accessible.
- Use `aria-label` for media with no visible text (e.g., `<video aria-label="Product demo video">`).

### Best Practices

- **File Organization**: Store media in a dedicated folder (e.g., `images/`, `videos/`) for maintainability.
- **Cross-Browser Testing**: Verify media compatibility across browsers (e.g., Safari may not support WebM).
- **Licensing**: Use royalty-free or properly licensed media to avoid legal issues.
- **Fallback Content**: Provide text or alternative content for unsupported browsers.

---

## 2.6 Hands-On Project: Build a Simple Personal Homepage

### Project Overview

This hands-on project guides you through creating a simple personal homepage using HTML, incorporating links, navigation, and multimedia. The homepage will feature a header with navigation, an about section with text and an image, and a footer. This project reinforces the concepts covered in Chapter 2, providing practical experience with HTML structure, semantic elements, links, and multimedia.

### Step 1: Setting Up the Project

Create a project folder named `personal-homepage` with the following structure:

personal-homepage/

├── images/

│ └── profile.jpg

├── index.html

```
├── about.html

├── styles.css
```

- Download a royalty-free image (e.g., from Unsplash) and save it as `profile.jpg` in the `images/` folder.
- Use Visual Studio Code and Live Server (set up in Chapter 1) to preview your work.

### Step 2: Creating the Homepage (`index.html`)

In `index.html`, add the following code to create a semantic structure with navigation and multimedia:

```
<!DOCTYPE html>

<html lang="en">

<head>

  <meta charset="UTF-8">

  <meta name="viewport" content="width=device-width, initial-scale=1.0">

  <title>My Personal Homepage</title>

  <link rel="stylesheet" href="styles.css">

</head>

<body>

  <header>

    <h1>Welcome to My Homepage</h1>

    <nav>

      <ul>
```

```
            <li><a href="index.html" aria-current="page">Home</a></li>

            <li><a href="about.html">About</a></li>

            <li><a href="#contact">Contact</a></li>

        </ul>

      </nav>

  </header>

  <main>

      <section id="about">

        <h2>About Me</h2>

        <p>Hello! I'm learning web development to create amazing websites. This is
my personal homepage, showcasing my skills and interests.</p>

        <figure>

            <img src="images/profile.jpg" alt="A profile photo of me smiling"
width="300">

            <figcaption>My Profile Photo</figcaption>

        </figure>

      </section>

      <section id="contact">

        <h2>Contact</h2>

        <p>Email me at <a
href="mailto:me@example.com">me@example.com</a>.</p>

      </section>

  </main>
```

```
    <footer>

        <p>&copy; 2025 My Homepage. All rights reserved.</p>

    </footer>

</body>

</html>
```

This includes:

- A semantic structure with `<header>`, `<nav>`, `<main>`, and `<footer>`.
- A navigation menu with internal and anchor links.
- An image with a `<figure>` and `<figcaption>` for semantic clarity.
- A contact section with an email link.

## Step 3: Creating the About Page (`about.html`)

In `about.html`, add:

```
<!DOCTYPE html>

<html lang="en">

<head>

    <meta charset="UTF-8">

    <meta name="viewport" content="width=device-width, initial-scale=1.0">

    <title>About Me</title>

    <link rel="stylesheet" href="styles.css">

</head>

<body>

    <header>
```

```
        <h1>About Me</h1>
        <nav>
            <ul>
                <li><a href="index.html">Home</a></li>
                <li><a href="about.html" aria-current="page">About</a></li>
                <li><a href="index.html#contact">Contact</a></li>
            </ul>
        </nav>
    </header>
    <main>
        <section>
            <h2>My Journey</h2>
            <p>I'm passionate about technology and design. I'm currently learning HTML, CSS, and JavaScript to build user-friendly websites.</p>
            <p>Check out this short introduction video:</p>
            <video controls width="600">
                <source src="https://example.com/intro.mp4" type="video/mp4">
                Your browser does not support the video tag.
            </video>
        </section>
    </main>
    <footer>
```

```
        <p>&copy; 2025 My Homepage. All rights reserved.</p>
    </footer>
</body>
</html>
```

Note: Replace the video `src` with a real video URL or a local file if available.

## Step 4: Styling with CSS (`styles.css`)

In `styles.css`, add:

```
body {
    font-family: Arial, sans-serif;
    margin: 0;
    padding: 20px;
    background-color: #f4f4f4;
}

header {
    background-color: #333;
    color: white;
    text-align: center;
    padding: 20px;
}
```

```
nav ul {
    list-style: none;
    padding: 0;
    display: flex;
    justify-content: center;
    gap: 20px;
}

nav a {
    color: white;
    text-decoration: none;
}

nav a:hover, nav a[aria-current="page"] {
    color: #007bff;
}

main {
    max-width: 800px;
    margin: 20px auto;
    background-color: white;
    padding: 20px;
```

```
    border-radius: 8px;
}

img {
    display: block;
    margin: 20px auto;
    max-width: 100%;
}

video {
    display: block;
    margin: 20px auto;
}

footer {
    text-align: center;
    margin-top: 20px;
    color: #666;
}
```

This CSS creates a clean, responsive design with a centered navigation menu, styled links, and a card-like main section.

## Step 5: Testing and Validation

- Open `index.html` with Live Server or a browser to test navigation between pages and the anchor link to the contact section.
- Verify the image and video (if used) load correctly.
- Check accessibility using a screen reader or the WAVE tool.
- Validate HTML with the W3C Markup Validator.

## Step 6: Enhancements

To extend the project:

- Add a portfolio section with more images.
- Include an `<audio>` element for background music or a podcast.
- Use CSS to make the navigation responsive (e.g., a hamburger menu for mobile).
- Deploy the site to GitHub Pages for public access.

# Chapter 3

# CSS – Styling Your Web Pages

## 3.1 Introduction to CSS: Bringing Your Pages to Life

### The Role of CSS in Web Development

Cascading Style Sheets (CSS) is the styling language of the web, responsible for transforming the raw structure of HTML into visually appealing and user-friendly webpages. While HTML provides the skeleton of a website, CSS adds the visual flair—colors, layouts, typography, and animations—that make it engaging and intuitive. CSS allows developers to control the appearance of elements across multiple pages, ensuring consistency and enhancing the user experience. As a core component of front-end development, CSS is essential for creating modern, responsive, and accessible websites.

Introduced in 1996 by the World Wide Web Consortium (W3C), CSS has evolved significantly, with CSS3 introducing advanced features like animations, transitions, and flexible layouts. CSS enables developers to separate content (HTML) from presentation (CSS), making websites easier to maintain and update. By mastering CSS, you can create visually stunning designs, adapt layouts for different devices, and bring creative ideas to life, making it a critical skill for web developers.

### Why CSS Matters

CSS is indispensable for several reasons:

- **Visual Appeal**: CSS transforms plain HTML into aesthetically pleasing designs, using colors, fonts, and layouts to engage users.
- **Consistency**: By applying styles across multiple pages, CSS ensures a uniform look and feel, reinforcing brand identity.
- **Responsiveness**: CSS enables responsive design, allowing websites to adapt seamlessly to desktops, tablets, and smartphones.

- **Accessibility**: Proper use of CSS enhances accessibility by ensuring readable fonts, sufficient color contrast, and clear visual hierarchies.
- **Efficiency**: External CSS files allow developers to update styles site-wide by editing a single file, reducing maintenance time.

For example, a single CSS rule can change the background color of all buttons on a website:

```
button {

  background-color: #007bff;

  color: white;

}
```

This efficiency and flexibility make CSS a powerful tool for web design.

## How CSS Works

CSS works by selecting HTML elements and applying styling rules to them. These rules are defined in a stylesheet, which can be:

- **External**: A separate `.css` file linked to HTML via `<link>` (e.g., `<link rel="stylesheet" href="styles.css">`).
- **Internal**: Embedded in the HTML `<head>` using a `<style>` tag.
- **Inline**: Applied directly to an element using the `style` attribute (e.g., `<p style="color: blue;">`).

External stylesheets are preferred for maintainability, as they allow styles to be reused across multiple pages. The “cascading” nature of CSS refers to how styles are applied based on priority and specificity, with more specific rules overriding general ones.

## CSS in the Modern Web

CSS3, the latest iteration, introduced features that have transformed web design:

- **Flexbox and Grid**: Layout systems for creating complex, responsive designs.

- **Animations and Transitions**: Smooth visual effects without JavaScript.
- **Media Queries**: Rules for adapting styles based on device characteristics (e.g., screen size).
- **Custom Properties (Variables)**: Reusable values for consistent styling (e.g., `--primary-color: #007bff;`).
- **Transforms**: Effects like rotation or scaling for dynamic visuals.

These features enable developers to create sophisticated designs, such as single-page applications or animated landing pages, without relying heavily on JavaScript or external libraries.

## Benefits of Learning CSS

Learning CSS offers numerous advantages:

- **Creative Expression**: CSS allows you to design unique interfaces, from minimalist blogs to vibrant e-commerce sites.
- **Career Opportunities**: Proficiency in CSS is a prerequisite for front-end development roles and enhances full-stack capabilities.
- **Cross-Device Compatibility**: CSS ensures websites look great on all devices, a critical skill in today's mobile-first world.
- **Collaboration with Designers**: CSS bridges the gap between design mockups (e.g., from Figma) and functional websites.
- **Community and Resources**: A vast ecosystem of tutorials, frameworks (e.g., Bootstrap, Tailwind CSS), and tools supports CSS learning.

## Getting Started with CSS

To start using CSS, you need:

- A text editor (e.g., Visual Studio Code) to write CSS rules.
- A browser with developer tools (e.g., Chrome DevTools) to inspect and test styles.
- An HTML file to apply styles to.

For example, create a simple HTML file (`index.html`):

```
<!DOCTYPE html>

<html lang="en">
```

```
<head>
    <meta charset="UTF-8">
    <title>CSS Example</title>
    <link rel="stylesheet" href="styles.css">
</head>
<body>
    <h1>Welcome</h1>
    <p>This is my first styled page.</p>
</body>
</html>
```

And a corresponding `styles.css`:

```
h1 {
    color: #333;
    text-align: center;
}
p {
    font-size: 18px;
    color: #666;
}
```

Open the HTML file in a browser to see the styled content.

### Challenges and Best Practices

CSS can be challenging due to browser compatibility issues or complex layouts, but best practices help:

- **Use External Stylesheets**: Keep CSS separate from HTML for maintainability.
- **Test Cross-Browser**: Ensure styles work in Chrome, Firefox, Safari, and Edge.
- **Optimize for Performance**: Minimize CSS file size using tools like CSSNano.
- **Follow Naming Conventions**: Use BEM (Block Element Modifier) or similar for organized class names.
- **Validate CSS**: Use the W3C CSS Validator to catch errors.

---

## 3.2 CSS Syntax and Selectors

### Understanding CSS Syntax

CSS syntax is straightforward yet powerful, consisting of rules that define how HTML elements are styled. Each rule comprises a selector and a declaration block:

```
selector {
  property: value;
}
```

- **Selector**: Targets the HTML element(s) to style (e.g., `h1`, `.class`, `#id`).
- **Declaration Block**: Enclosed in curly braces `{}`, contains one or more declarations.
- **Declaration**: A property-value pair (e.g., `color: blue;`), separated by a colon and ending with a semicolon.

Example:

```
p {
    font-size: 16px;
    color: #333;
}
```

This rule targets all `<p>` elements, setting their font size to 16 pixels and text color to a dark gray.

## Types of CSS Selectors

Selectors are the mechanism by which CSS targets HTML elements. Understanding selectors is crucial for precise and efficient styling. Common selector types include:

### 1. Element Selectors

Target elements by their tag name:

```
div {
    background-color: #f0f0f0;
}
```

This styles all `<div>` elements.

### 2. Class Selectors

Target elements with a specific class attribute, prefixed with a dot (`.`):

```
.intro {
    font-weight: bold;
}
```

Applies to elements like `<p class="intro">`. Classes are reusable and can be applied to multiple elements.

**3. ID Selectors**

Target a single element with a unique ID, prefixed with a hash (`#`):

```
#main {
   width: 100%;
}
```

Applies to `<div id="main">`. IDs should be unique per page.

**4. Attribute Selectors**

Target elements based on their attributes:

```
input[type="text"] {
   border: 1px solid #ccc;
}
```

Styles `<input>` elements with `type="text"`.

**5. Pseudo-Classes and Pseudo-Elements**

**Pseudo-Classes**: Style elements based on state or position (e.g., `:hover`, `:first-child`):

```
a:hover {
   color: #007bff;
}
```

•

**Pseudo-Elements**: Style specific parts of an element (e.g., `::before`, `::after`):

```
p::first-line {

  font-weight: bold;

}
```

•

**6. Combinators**

Combine selectors to target elements based on their relationships:

**Descendant Selector** (space): Targets elements nested within another:

```
nav a {

  text-decoration: none;

}
```

•

**Child Selector** (`>`): Targets direct children:

```
ul > li {

  margin-bottom: 10px;

}
```

•

**Adjacent Sibling Selector** (`+`): Targets the next sibling:

```
h2 + p {

  margin-top: 0;

}
```

•

**General Sibling Selector** (~): Targets all subsequent siblings:

```
h2 ~ p {

   color: #666;

}
```

- 

**7. Universal Selector**

Targets all elements:

```
* {

   box-sizing: border-box;

}
```

Use sparingly due to performance implications.

## Specificity and the Cascade

The “cascading” in CSS refers to how the browser determines which styles to apply when multiple rules target the same element. This is governed by:

- **Specificity**: Selectors with higher specificity take precedence. Specificity is calculated based on the selector type (ID > class > element). For example, `#main` is more specific than `.intro`, which is more specific than `div`.
- **Order**: If specificity is equal, the last rule in the stylesheet wins.
- **!important**: Overrides other rules (e.g., `color: red !important;`), but should be used sparingly to avoid maintenance issues.

Example:

```
p {

   color: blue;

}
```

```
.intro {

  color: red;

}
```

A `<p class="intro">` will be red because `.intro` has higher specificity.

## Organizing CSS Rules

To maintain clean CSS:

- **Group Related Rules**: Organize styles by section (e.g., header, main, footer).

**Use Comments**: Add comments to explain sections:

```
/* Navigation Styles */

nav {

  background-color: #333;

}
```

-

**Modularize with Frameworks**: Use CSS frameworks like BEM for consistent naming:

```
.block__element--modifier {

  font-size: 14px;

}
```

-

## Advanced Selectors

CSS3 introduced advanced selectors like:

- **:nth-child(n)**: Targets elements based on their position (e.g., `li:nth-child(2)`).
- **:not(selector)**: Excludes elements (e.g., `button:not(.disabled)`).

**:where() and :is()**: Group selectors for cleaner code:

```
:is(h1, h2, h3) {

  font-family: Arial;

}
```

-

### Best Practices

- **Avoid Overly Specific Selectors**: Use `.class` over nested selectors like `div ul li a` for maintainability.
- **Minimize !important**: Reserve for rare cases to avoid specificity conflicts.
- **Test Responsiveness**: Use media queries to adjust selectors for different devices.
- **Validate CSS**: Use the W3C CSS Validator to ensure correctness.

---

## 3.3 Working with Colors, Fonts, and Text Styling

### The Importance of Colors and Typography

Colors, fonts, and text styling are central to web design, influencing user perception, readability, and engagement. Colors set the mood and reinforce brand identity, while typography ensures content is legible and visually appealing. CSS provides a robust set of properties to control these elements, allowing developers to create cohesive and accessible designs. This section explores how to use CSS to manage colors, fonts, and text styling, with a focus on best practices for usability and aesthetics.

### Working with Colors

CSS supports multiple ways to specify colors:

- **Named Colors**: Simple keywords like `red`, `blue`, or `transparent` (147 predefined names).
- **Hexadecimal**: A six-digit code (e.g., `#ff0000` for red) or shorthand (e.g., `#f00`).
- **RGB/RGBA**: Defines red, green, blue values (0-255), with optional alpha for opacity (e.g., `rgb(255, 0, 0)` or `rgba(255, 0, 0, 0.5)`).
- **HSL/HSLA**: Specifies hue, saturation, lightness, and optional alpha (e.g., `hsl(0, 100%, 50%)`).
- **CSS Variables**: Reusable color values (e.g., `--primary: #007bff;`).

Example:

```
body {

  background-color: #f4f4f4;

  color: rgb(51, 51, 51);

}

button {

  background-color: var(--primary);

}
```

**Color Best Practices**

- **Contrast for Accessibility**: Ensure sufficient contrast between text and background (WCAG recommends a 4.5:1 ratio for normal text). Use tools like WebAIM's Contrast Checker.

**Consistent Palette**: Define a color scheme (e.g., primary, secondary, accent colors) using CSS variables:

```
:root {

  --primary: #007bff;

  --secondary: #6c757d;
```

}

- 
- **Semantic Colors**: Use colors to convey meaning (e.g., red for errors, green for success).

## Working with Fonts

CSS controls typography through font-related properties:

- **font-family**: Specifies the typeface (e.g., `font-family: Arial, sans-serif;`).
- **font-size**: Sets text size (e.g., `font-size: 16px;` or `font-size: 1rem;`).
- **font-weight**: Controls boldness (e.g., `font-weight: 400;` or `font-weight: bold;`).
- **font-style**: Sets italic or normal (e.g., `font-style: italic;`).
- **line-height**: Adjusts spacing between lines (e.g., `line-height: 1.5;` for 1.5 times the font size).

Example:

```
h1 {

  font-family: "Roboto", sans-serif;

  font-size: 2.5rem;

  font-weight: 700;

  line-height: 1.2;

}
```

### Web-Safe Fonts and Custom Fonts

- **Web-Safe Fonts**: Fonts like Arial, Times New Roman, and Helvetica are universally available.

**Google Fonts**: Free, easy-to-use fonts linked via `<link>` or `@import`:

```
<link
href="https://fonts.googleapis.com/css2?family=Roboto:wght@400;700&display=swap" rel="stylesheet">
```

- 

**Custom Fonts**: Use `@font-face` to load custom fonts:

```
@font-face {
  font-family: "CustomFont";
  src: url("custom-font.woff2") format("woff2");
}
```

- 

**Font Best Practices**

- **Fallback Fonts**: Always include fallback fonts (e.g., `font-family: "Roboto", sans-serif;`).
- **Readable Sizes**: Use relative units like `rem` or `em` for scalability (e.g., `font-size: 1rem;`).
- **Optimize Loading**: Use `font-display: swap;` in `@font-face` to prevent text blocking during font loading.

## Text Styling Properties

CSS offers properties to enhance text appearance:

- **text-align**: Aligns text (e.g., `text-align: center;`).
- **text-decoration**: Adds underlines, overlines, or strikethroughs (e.g., `text-decoration: underline;`).
- **text-transform**: Changes case (e.g., `text-transform: uppercase;`).
- **letter-spacing**: Adjusts space between characters (e.g., `letter-spacing: 1px;`).
- **word-spacing**: Adjusts space between words (e.g., `word-spacing: 2px;`).

- **text-shadow**: Adds shadows (e.g., `text-shadow: 2px 2px 4px rgba(0, 0, 0, 0.3);`).

Example:

```
p {
  text-align: justify;
  text-decoration: none;
  letter-spacing: 0.5px;
  text-shadow: 1px 1px 2px rgba(0, 0, 0, 0.1);
}
```

## Accessibility and Usability

- **Contrast and Readability**: Ensure text is legible against backgrounds (e.g., dark text on light backgrounds).

**Responsive Typography**: Use relative units (`rem`, `vw`) to scale text for different screen sizes:

```
@media (max-width: 600px) {
  h1 {
    font-size: 1.5rem;
  }
}
```

- 
- **Avoid Overstyling**: Excessive decorations (e.g., heavy shadows) can reduce readability.

## Combining Colors and Typography

A cohesive design combines colors and typography:

```
:root {
   --primary: #007bff;
   --text: #333;
}
header {
   background-color: var(--primary);
   color: white;
   font-family: "Roboto", sans-serif;
   text-align: center;
   padding: 20px;
}
p {
   color: var(--text);
   font-size: 1rem;
   line-height: 1.6;
}
```

## Testing and Tools

- **Browser DevTools**: Use Chrome DevTools to experiment with colors and fonts in real-time.
- **Color Pickers**: Tools like Coolors or Adobe Color help create harmonious palettes.

- **Typography Tools**: Use WhatTheFont or FontSquirrel Matcherator to identify fonts.
- **Validation**: Test with WAVE or Lighthouse for accessibility compliance.

# 3.4 Box Model: Margins, Padding, and Borders

## Understanding the CSS Box Model

The CSS box model is a fundamental concept that defines how elements are structured and spaced on a webpage. Every HTML element is treated as a rectangular box, consisting of content, padding, borders, and margins. These components determine the element's size, spacing, and positioning, making the box model essential for creating consistent and visually appealing layouts. By mastering the box model, developers can control the spacing and appearance of elements, ensuring precise and responsive designs.

## Components of the Box Model

The box model consists of four layers:

- **Content**: The core content of the element, such as text or images, defined by its `width` and `height`.
- **Padding**: The space between the content and the border, controlled by the `padding` property.
- **Border**: A line surrounding the padding, controlled by the `border` property.
- **Margin**: The outer space around the border, separating the element from others, controlled by the `margin` property.

The total size of an element is calculated as:

Total Width = width + padding-left + padding-right + border-left + border-right + margin-left + margin-right

Total Height = height + padding-top + padding-bottom + border-top + border-bottom + margin-top + margin-bottom

For example, an element with `width: 200px`, `padding: 10px`, `border: 2px`, and `margin: 20px` has a total width of `200 + 10 + 10 + 2 + 2 + 20 + 20 = 264px`.

## Box-Sizing Property

The `box-sizing` property controls how the `width` and `height` are calculated:

- **content-box** (default): `width` and `height` apply only to the content, excluding padding and border.
- **border-box**: `width` and `height` include content, padding, and border, making calculations simpler.

Using `border-box` is a best practice for predictable layouts:

```
* {
  box-sizing: border-box;
}
```

This ensures that padding and borders are included in the specified `width` and `height`, preventing unexpected overflow.

## Padding

Padding creates space inside the element, between the content and the border. It can be set using:

- **Shorthand**: `padding: 10px;` (applies to all sides).
- **Individual Sides**: `padding-top: 10px; padding-right: 15px; padding-bottom: 10px; padding-left: 15px;`.
- **Two Values**: `padding: 10px 20px;` (top/bottom, left/right).
- **Four Values**: `padding: 10px 20px 30px 40px;` (top, right, bottom, left).

Example:

```
div {
```

```
    padding: 20px;

    background-color: #f0f0f0;

}
```

Padding enhances readability by providing breathing room around content.

## Borders

The `border` property defines a line around the padding, with sub-properties:

- **border-width**: Thickness (e.g., `border-width: 2px;`).
- **border-style**: Style (e.g., `solid`, `dashed`, `dotted`).
- **border-color**: Color (e.g., `border-color: #333;`).
- **Shorthand**: `border: 2px solid #333;`.

Example:

```
button {

    border: 1px solid #007bff;

    border-radius: 5px;

}
```

The `border-radius` property rounds corners, enhancing visual appeal.

## Margins

Margins create space outside the border, separating elements. Like padding, margins can be set using shorthand or individual properties:

```
div {

    margin: 20px;
```

```
}
```

Margins can also be negative to overlap elements or use `auto` for centering:

```
.container {
    width: 800px;
    margin: 0 auto;
}
```

## Margin Collapse

A unique feature of margins is **margin collapse**, where adjacent vertical margins combine into the larger of the two. For example:

```
div.top {
    margin-bottom: 20px;
}
div.bottom {
    margin-top: 30px;
}
```

The space between `div.top` and `div.bottom` will be 30px, not 50px. Margin collapse applies only to vertical margins and can be avoided using padding or CSS layouts like Flexbox.

## Practical Applications

The box model is used to:

- **Create Spacing**: Ensure elements are well-separated for readability.
- **Control Layout**: Align elements using margins (e.g., centering with `margin: auto`).
- **Enhance Visuals**: Use borders and padding to create buttons, cards, or containers.
- **Prevent Overflow**: Use `box-sizing: border-box` to manage element sizes.

Example of a styled card:

```
.card {
  width: 300px;
  padding: 20px;
  border: 1px solid #ccc;
  margin: 15px;
  border-radius: 8px;
  box-sizing: border-box;
}
```

## Accessibility and Best Practices

- **Ensure Readability**: Use sufficient padding to avoid cramped content.
- **Maintain Consistency**: Apply uniform margins and padding for a cohesive design.

**Test Responsiveness**: Adjust margins and padding for different screen sizes using media queries:

```
@media (max-width: 600px) {
  .card {
    margin: 10px;
```

```
        padding: 15px;
    }
}
```

- 
- **Avoid Excessive Margins**: Overuse can lead to unnecessary whitespace or layout issues.

**Use CSS Resets**: Normalize default margins and padding across browsers:

```
* {
    margin: 0;
    padding: 0;
    box-sizing: border-box;
}
```

- 

## Debugging the Box Model

Use browser developer tools (e.g., Chrome DevTools) to inspect the box model. The "Layout" or "Box Model" view shows content, padding, borders, and margins visually, helping identify spacing issues. Common problems include:

- Unexpected overflow due to `content-box`.
- Margin collapse causing inconsistent spacing.
- Incorrect border styles affecting design.

---

# 3.5 Layout Techniques: Flexbox and Grid Basics

## The Evolution of CSS Layouts

Creating layouts is a core aspect of web design, and CSS provides powerful tools like Flexbox and Grid to build flexible, responsive structures. Before their introduction in CSS3, layouts relied on techniques like floats and positioning, which were often cumbersome and error-prone. Flexbox and Grid offer intuitive, efficient ways to arrange elements, making it easier to create complex, adaptive designs. This section introduces the basics of Flexbox and Grid, explaining their properties, use cases, and best practices for modern web development.

## Flexbox: Flexible Box Layout

Flexbox is a one-dimensional layout system designed for arranging elements in a row or column. It excels at distributing space and aligning items within a container, making it ideal for navigation menus, card layouts, and responsive designs.

### Key Flexbox Concepts

- **Flex Container**: The parent element with `display: flex;` or `display: inline-flex;`.
- **Flex Items**: The child elements inside the flex container.

To create a flex layout:

```
.container {
  display: flex;
}
```

### Flexbox Properties

**flex-direction**: Defines the main axis (e.g., `row`, `column`, `row-reverse`):

```
.container {
  flex-direction: row;
```

}

- 

**justify-content**: Aligns items along the main axis (e.g., `flex-start`, `center`, `space-between`, `space-around`):

```
.container {

  justify-content: space-between;

}
```

- 

**align-items**: Aligns items along the cross axis (e.g., `flex-start`, `center`, `stretch`):

```
.container {

  align-items: center;

}
```

- 

**flex-wrap**: Controls whether items wrap to new lines (e.g., `nowrap`, `wrap`):

```
.container {

  flex-wrap: wrap;

}
```

- 

**flex**: Shorthand for item properties (`flex-grow`, `flex-shrink`, `flex-basis`):

```
.item {

  flex: 1;

}
```

- 

Example: A responsive navigation bar:

```
.nav {

    display: flex;

    justify-content: space-around;

    align-items: center;

    flex-wrap: wrap;

}

.nav a {

    padding: 10px;

}
```

### Use Cases

- Navigation menus with evenly spaced links.
- Centering content vertically and horizontally.
- Responsive layouts where items adjust based on available space.

## Grid: CSS Grid Layout

Grid is a two-dimensional layout system for arranging elements in rows and columns. It's ideal for complex layouts, such as dashboards or magazine-style pages, where precise control over both axes is needed.

### Key Grid Concepts

- **Grid Container**: The parent element with `display: grid;`.
- **Grid Items**: The child elements placed in the grid.
- **Grid Lines**: The lines defining rows and columns.
- **Grid Tracks**: The rows or columns themselves.

To create a grid:

```
.container {

  display: grid;

}
```

**Grid Properties**

**grid-template-columns/rows**: Defines the size of columns or rows:

```
.container {

  grid-template-columns: 1fr 2fr 1fr;

}
```

- Here, `1fr` (fractional unit) divides available space proportionally.

**gap**: Sets spacing between grid items:

```
.container {

  gap: 20px;

}
```

- 

**grid-area**: Assigns items to specific grid areas:

```
.item {

  grid-area: 1 / 1 / 2 / 3;

}
```

- 

**justify-items/align-items**: Aligns items within cells:

```
.container {

  justify-items: center;

  align-items: center;
```

```
}
```

- 

Example: A simple grid layout:

```
.grid {
    display: grid;
    grid-template-columns: repeat(3, 1fr);
    gap: 10px;
}
.grid-item {
    background-color: #f0f0f0;
    padding: 20px;
}
```

**Use Cases**

- Complex layouts with headers, sidebars, and content areas.
- Responsive galleries with equal-sized items.
- Dashboard designs with precise positioning.

## Combining Flexbox and Grid

Flexbox and Grid complement each other:

- Use **Flexbox** for one-dimensional layouts (e.g., navigation bars, single rows/columns).
- Use **Grid** for two-dimensional layouts (e.g., page layouts with multiple sections).
- Combine them for nested layouts (e.g., a Grid container with Flexbox items).

Example:

```
<div class="grid">

    <div class="flex-item">

        <div class="flex">Item 1</div>

        <div class="flex">Item 2</div>

    </div>

</div>


.grid {

    display: grid;

    grid-template-columns: 1fr 1fr;

}

.flex-item {

    display: flex;

    justify-content: space-between;

}
```

## Responsive Design

Both Flexbox and Grid support responsive design:

**Media Queries**: Adjust layouts based on screen size:

```
@media (max-width: 600px) {

    .grid {

        grid-template-columns: 1fr;
```

```
    }
}
```

•

**Auto-Fit and Minmax**: Create flexible grids:

```
.grid {
    grid-template-columns: repeat(auto-fit, minmax(200px, 1fr));
}
```

•

### Best Practices

- **Start Simple**: Begin with basic Flexbox or Grid layouts before combining them.
- **Test Responsiveness**: Use browser dev tools to simulate different screen sizes.
- **Use Semantic HTML**: Pair layouts with semantic elements like `<nav>` or `<main>`.
- **Optimize Performance**: Avoid overly complex grids that slow rendering.
- **Leverage Browser Support**: Both Flexbox and Grid are widely supported, but test on older browsers if needed.

---

## 3.6 Hands-On Project: Style a Blog Page

### Project Overview

This hands-on project guides you through styling a blog page using CSS, incorporating the box model, Flexbox, and Grid, along with colors, fonts, and text styling. The blog page will feature a header with navigation, a main section with blog posts, a sidebar, and a footer. This project reinforces the concepts from Chapter 3, providing practical experience in creating a visually appealing, responsive layout.

### Step 1: Setting Up the Project

Create a folder named `blog-page` with the following structure:

```
blog-page/
├── images/
│   └── post-image.jpg
├── index.html
├── styles.css
```

- Download a royalty-free image (e.g., from Unsplash) and save it as `post-image.jpg` in the `images/` folder.
- Use Visual Studio Code and Live Server to preview your work.

## Step 2: Creating the HTML (`index.html`)

In `index.html`, add:

```html
<!DOCTYPE html>
<html lang="en">
<head>
  <meta charset="UTF-8">
  <meta name="viewport" content="width=device-width, initial-scale=1.0">
  <title>My Blog</title>
  <link rel="stylesheet" href="styles.css">
</head>
<body>
  <header>
```

```
        <h1>My Blog</h1>

        <nav>

            <ul>

                <li><a href="#" aria-current="page">Home</a></li>

                <li><a href="#">About</a></li>

                <li><a href="#">Contact</a></li>

            </ul>

        </nav>

    </header>

    <div class="container">

        <main>

            <article class="post">

                <h2>Blog Post Title</h2>

                <p class="meta">Posted on September 19, 2025</p>

                <img src="images/post-image.jpg" alt="A scenic landscape">

                <p>Lorem ipsum dolor sit amet, consectetur adipiscing elit. Sed do eiusmod tempor incididunt ut labore et dolore magna aliqua.</p>

            </article>

            <article class="post">

                <h2>Another Post</h2>

                <p class="meta">Posted on September 18, 2025</p>

                <p>Ut enim ad minim veniam, quis nostrud exercitation ullamco laboris nisi ut aliquip ex ea commodo consequat.</p>
```

```
            </article>
        </main>
        <aside>
            <h3>About the Author</h3>
            <p>I'm a web developer passionate about creating engaging content.</p>
        </aside>
    </div>
    <footer>
        <p>&copy; 2025 My Blog. All rights reserved.</p>
    </footer>
</body>
</html>
```

This HTML uses semantic elements (<header>, <nav>, <main>, <article>, <aside>, <footer>) and includes a navigation menu, blog posts with an image, and a sidebar.

### Step 3: Styling with CSS (styles.css)

In styles.css, add:

```
/* Reset and Box Model */
* {
    box-sizing: border-box;
    margin: 0;
```

```
    padding: 0;
}

/* Root Variables */
:root {
    --primary: #007bff;
    --text: #333;
    --background: #f4f4f4;
}

/* Body */
body {
    font-family: 'Roboto', Arial, sans-serif;
    background-color: var(--background);
    color: var(--text);
    line-height: 1.6;
}

/* Header */
header {
    background-color: var(--primary);
    color: white;
```

```
    text-align: center;
    padding: 20px;
    margin-bottom: 20px;
}

header h1 {
    font-size: 2.5rem;
    margin-bottom: 10px;
}

nav ul {
    display: flex;
    justify-content: center;
    gap: 20px;
    list-style: none;
}

nav a {
    color: white;
    text-decoration: none;
    font-weight: 500;
}
```

```
nav a:hover, nav a[aria-current="page"] {

    color: #f0f0f0;

}


/* Main Container (Grid) */

.container {

    display: grid;

    grid-template-columns: 2fr 1fr;

    gap: 20px;

    max-width: 1000px;

    margin: 0 auto;

    padding: 0 20px;

}


/* Main Content */

main {

    display: flex;

    flex-direction: column;

    gap: 20px;

}
```

```
.post {
    background-color: white;
    padding: 20px;
    border: 1px solid #ccc;
    border-radius: 8px;
}

.post h2 {
    font-size: 1.8rem;
    margin-bottom: 10px;
}

.post .meta {
    font-size: 0.9rem;
    color: #666;
    margin-bottom: 10px;
}

.post img {
    max-width: 100%;
    height: auto;
    margin: 15px 0;
```

```
    border-radius: 5px;
}

/* Sidebar */
aside {
    background-color: white;
    padding: 20px;
    border: 1px solid #ccc;
    border-radius: 8px;
}

aside h3 {
    font-size: 1.5rem;
    margin-bottom: 10px;
}

/* Footer */
footer {
    text-align: center;
    padding: 20px;
    margin-top: 20px;
    color: #666;
```

```
}


/* Responsive Design */
@media (max-width: 768px) {
  .container {
    grid-template-columns: 1fr;
  }
  header h1 {
    font-size: 2rem;
  }
  nav ul {
    flex-direction: column;
    align-items: center;
  }
}
```

This CSS:

- Uses a CSS reset and `box-sizing: border-box`.
- Defines color variables for consistency.
- Styles the header with a Flexbox navigation menu.
- Uses Grid for the main layout (main content and sidebar).
- Applies Flexbox for blog posts within `<main>`.
- Styles the box model (margins, padding, borders) for posts and sidebar.
- Includes responsive design with a media query for mobile devices.

## Step 4: Testing and Validation

- Open `index.html` with Live Server to verify the layout, navigation, and image display.
- Test responsiveness by resizing the browser or using DevTools' device mode.
- Check accessibility with WAVE or Lighthouse, ensuring sufficient contrast and keyboard navigation.
- Validate CSS with the W3C CSS Validator.

## Step 5: Enhancements

To extend the project:

- Add hover effects to blog posts (e.g., `box-shadow` on hover).
- Include a second image or video in a post.
- Use Google Fonts for custom typography.
- Deploy to GitHub Pages for public access.

# Chapter 4

# JavaScript – Adding Interactivity

## 4.1 What is JavaScript? The Power of Dynamic Websites

### The Role of JavaScript in Web Development

JavaScript is a versatile, high-level programming language that brings interactivity and dynamism to websites, transforming static HTML and CSS into engaging, responsive experiences. Often referred to as the "language of the web," JavaScript enables developers to create features like interactive forms, real-time updates, animations, and complex web applications. While HTML structures content and CSS styles it, JavaScript adds behavior, allowing websites to respond to user actions, fetch data, and update content without reloading the page. As a core pillar of front-end development, JavaScript is essential for building modern, user-friendly websites and applications.

Initially developed by Brendan Eich in 1995 under the codename "Mocha" at Netscape, JavaScript has evolved into a robust language standardized as ECMAScript (ES). The release of ES6 (2015) and subsequent updates introduced features like arrow functions, promises, and modules, making JavaScript more powerful and developer-friendly. Today, JavaScript powers not only browsers but also server-side applications (via Node.js), mobile apps, and even desktop applications, cementing its role as a cornerstone of modern development.

### Why JavaScript Matters

JavaScript's significance stems from its ability to enhance user experience and enable complex functionality:

- **Interactivity**: JavaScript allows websites to respond to user inputs, such as clicks, form submissions, or mouse movements, creating engaging interfaces.
- **Dynamic Content**: It enables real-time updates, like loading new posts on a social media feed without refreshing the page.

- **Versatility**: JavaScript runs in browsers, on servers (Node.js), and in hybrid frameworks (e.g., React Native), making it a multi-platform language.
- **Rich Ecosystems**: Libraries like React, Vue.js, and Angular, along with tools like Webpack and Vite, extend JavaScript's capabilities for building sophisticated applications.
- **Universal Support**: All modern browsers (Chrome, Firefox, Safari, Edge) support JavaScript, ensuring broad compatibility.

For example, a simple JavaScript function can display a greeting when a button is clicked:

```
<button onclick="showGreeting()">Click Me</button>

<script>

  function showGreeting() {

    alert("Hello, welcome to my website!");

  }

</script>
```

This interactivity makes websites feel alive and responsive, enhancing user engagement.

## How JavaScript Works

JavaScript is a client-side scripting language executed by the browser's JavaScript engine (e.g., V8 in Chrome, SpiderMonkey in Firefox). When a webpage loads, the browser parses the HTML, builds the Document Object Model (DOM), and executes any JavaScript code. JavaScript can:

- Manipulate the DOM to change content, styles, or structure dynamically.
- Handle events like clicks, keypresses, or scrolling.
- Communicate with servers via APIs to fetch or send data.

JavaScript can be included in HTML in three ways:

- **Inline**: Using the `onclick` attribute (e.g., `<button onclick="myFunction()">`).
- **Internal**: Inside a `<script>` tag in the HTML `<head>` or `<body>`.
- **External**: In a separate `.js` file linked via `<script src="script.js"></script>`.

External scripts are preferred for maintainability and reusability:

```
<script src="script.js"></script>
```

## JavaScript in the Modern Web

Modern JavaScript powers a wide range of applications:

- **Single-Page Applications (SPAs)**: Frameworks like React and Vue.js use JavaScript to create fast, app-like experiences (e.g., Gmail, Netflix).
- **Progressive Web Apps (PWAs)**: JavaScript enables offline functionality and app-like behavior on the web.
- **Real-Time Features**: Technologies like WebSockets and libraries like Socket.IO enable live updates, such as chat apps or stock tickers.
- **Animations**: JavaScript, combined with CSS or libraries like GSAP, creates smooth animations and transitions.

For example, JavaScript can fetch data from an API and display it:

```
fetch('https://api.example.com/data')

  .then(response => response.json())

  .then(data => console.log(data));
```

## Benefits of Learning JavaScript

Learning JavaScript offers numerous advantages:

- **Essential for Web Development**: It's a core skill for front-end, back-end (with Node.js), and full-stack roles.

- **High Demand**: JavaScript developers are in demand, with opportunities in startups, tech giants, and freelance markets.
- **Creative Freedom**: JavaScript enables developers to build interactive features, games, and visualizations.
- **Community and Resources**: A vast ecosystem of tutorials, forums (e.g., Stack Overflow), and libraries supports learning.
- **Future-Proof**: JavaScript's ongoing evolution ensures its relevance in emerging technologies like Web3 and serverless architectures.

## Getting Started with JavaScript

To begin, you need:

- A text editor (e.g., Visual Studio Code) to write JavaScript.
- A browser with developer tools to test and debug (e.g., Chrome DevTools' Console).
- An HTML file to integrate JavaScript.

Start with simple scripts:

```
console.log("Hello, JavaScript!");
```

Experiment in the browser's console or use online editors like CodePen.

## Challenges and Best Practices

JavaScript can be challenging due to its asynchronous nature, browser quirks, or debugging complexity. Best practices include:

- **Use External Scripts**: Keep JavaScript separate from HTML for maintainability.
- **Write Clean Code**: Use meaningful variable names and comments.
- **Test Cross-Browser**: Ensure compatibility across Chrome, Firefox, and Safari.
- **Debug Effectively**: Use `console.log()` and browser dev tools to troubleshoot.
- **Stay Updated**: Follow ES updates (e.g., ES2023) for modern features.

---

# 4.2 JavaScript Basics: Variables, Data Types, and Functions

## The Building Blocks of JavaScript

JavaScript's power lies in its ability to manipulate data and define behaviors through variables, data types, and functions. These foundational concepts allow developers to store information, perform operations, and create reusable code, forming the basis for interactive web features. Understanding variables, data types, and functions is essential for writing effective JavaScript, enabling you to build dynamic and functional webpages.

## Variables

Variables store data for use in a program. JavaScript offers three ways to declare variables:

- **var**: Older method, function-scoped, with issues like hoisting (e.g., `var x = 5;`).
- **let**: Block-scoped, allows reassignment, preferred for modern code (e.g., `let count = 10;`).
- **const**: Block-scoped, cannot be reassigned after declaration (e.g., `const name = "Alice";`).

Example:

let age = 25;

const username = "John";

age = 26; // Valid

username = "Jane"; // Error: Assignment to constant

Best practices:

- Use `let` for variables that change, `const` for constants.

- Avoid `var` to prevent scoping issues.
- Use meaningful names (e.g., `userAge` instead of `x`).

## Data Types

JavaScript is dynamically typed, meaning variables can hold any data type without explicit declaration. Key data types include:

- **Primitive Types**:
  - **Number**: Integers or floats (e.g., `42`, `3.14`).
  - **String**: Text enclosed in quotes (e.g., `"Hello"`, `'World'`).
  - **Boolean**: `true` or `false`.
  - **Undefined**: A variable with no value (e.g., `let x;`).
  - **Null**: Represents no value (e.g., `let y = null;`).
  - **Symbol**: Unique identifiers (e.g., `const id = Symbol('id');`).
  - **BigInt**: For large integers (e.g., `123456789n`).
- **Non-Primitive Types**:
  - **Object**: Key-value pairs (e.g., `const user = { name: "Alice", age: 25 };`).
  - **Array**: Ordered lists (e.g., `const numbers = [1, 2, 3];`).
  - **Function**: Reusable code blocks (covered below).

Example:

```
let num = 42; // Number

let greeting = "Hello, World!"; // String

let isActive = true; // Boolean

let user = { name: "Alice", age: 25 }; // Object

let numbers = [1, 2, 3]; // Array
```

### Type Coercion

JavaScript automatically converts types in certain operations, which can lead to unexpected results:

```
console.log("5" + 3); // "53" (string concatenation)

console.log("5" - 3); // 2 (number subtraction)
```

Use explicit conversion with `parseInt()`, `parseFloat()`, or `String()` to avoid errors.

## Functions

Functions are reusable blocks of code that perform specific tasks. They can take inputs (parameters) and return outputs.

### Declaring Functions

**Function Declaration**:

```
function greet(name) {

   return `Hello, ${name}!`;

}

console.log(greet("Alice")); // "Hello, Alice!"
```

- 

**Function Expression**:

```
const add = function(a, b) {

   return a + b;

};

console.log(add(2, 3)); // 5
```

- 

**Arrow Functions** (ES6):

```
const multiply = (a, b) => a * b;

console.log(multiply(4, 5)); // 20
```

•

**Parameters and Return**

- Parameters are variables in the function definition (e.g., `name` in `greet(name)`).
- The `return` statement sends a value back; without it, the function returns `undefined`.

Default parameters (ES6) provide fallback values:

```
function welcome(user = "Guest") {

  return `Welcome, ${user}!`;

}

console.log(welcome()); // "Welcome, Guest!"
```

•

**Scope**

- **Global Scope**: Variables declared outside functions are accessible everywhere.
- **Local Scope**: Variables declared inside functions (with `let` or `const`) are only accessible within that function.
- **Block Scope**: `let` and `const` are limited to the block (e.g., inside `{}`).

Example:

```
let globalVar = "I'm global";

function testScope() {

  let localVar = "I'm local";

  console.log(globalVar); // Accessible

  console.log(localVar); // Accessible

}
```

console.log(localVar); // Error: localVar is not defined

### Common Operations

- **Arithmetic**: `+`, `-`, `*`, `/`, `%` (modulus).
- **String Concatenation**: Using `+` or template literals (`` `Hello, ${name}` ``).
- **Array Methods**: `push()`, `pop()`, `map()`, `filter()` (e.g., `numbers.map(n => n * 2)`).
- **Object Access**: Dot notation (`user.name`) or bracket notation (`user["name"]`).

Example:

```
const numbers = [1, 2, 3];

const doubled = numbers.map(num => num * 2); // [2, 4, 6]

const user = { name: "Bob", age: 30 };

console.log(user.name); // "Bob"
```

## Best Practices

- **Use `const` by Default**: Switch to `let` only when reassignment is needed.
- **Avoid Implicit Coercion**: Use explicit type conversion for clarity.
- **Write Modular Functions**: Keep functions small and focused on one task.

**Comment Code**: Explain complex logic with comments:

```
// Calculate total price with tax

function calculateTotal(price, taxRate = 0.1) {

  return price * (1 + taxRate);

}
```

- 

- **Debug with Console**: Use `console.log()`, `console.error()`, or `debugger`.

---

# 4.3 Manipulating the DOM: Making Pages Interactive

## What is the DOM?

The Document Object Model (DOM) is a programming interface that represents an HTML document as a tree of objects, allowing JavaScript to interact with and modify its structure, content, and styles dynamically. Each HTML element becomes a node in the DOM tree, accessible via JavaScript for manipulation. DOM manipulation is the heart of interactive web development, enabling features like updating text, adding elements, or responding to user actions without reloading the page.

## Accessing the DOM

JavaScript provides methods to select DOM elements:

**getElementById**: Selects an element by its `id`:
const header = document.getElementById('header');

-

**querySelector**: Selects the first element matching a CSS selector:
const firstPara = document.querySelector('p');

-

**querySelectorAll**: Returns a NodeList of all matching elements:
const allLinks = document.querySelectorAll('a');

-

Example:

<div id="content">Hello</div>

```
<script>

  const content = document.getElementById('content');

  console.log(content.textContent); // "Hello"

</script>
```

## Modifying the DOM

JavaScript can change the DOM in several ways:

**Content**: Update text or HTML:

```
content.textContent = "Welcome!";

content.innerHTML = "<strong>Welcome!</strong>";
```

- 

**Styles**: Modify CSS properties:

```
content.style.backgroundColor = "blue";

content.style.color = "white";
```

- 

**Attributes**: Change attributes like `src` or `class`:

```
const img = document.querySelector('img');

img.src = "new-image.jpg";

img.setAttribute('alt', 'New description');
```

- 

**Classes**: Add, remove, or toggle classes:

```
content.classList.add('highlight');

content.classList.remove('highlight');

content.classList.toggle('highlight');
```

- 

## Creating and Removing Elements

**Create Elements**:

```
const newPara = document.createElement('p');

newPara.textContent = "New paragraph";

document.body.appendChild(newPara);
```

- 

**Remove Elements**:

```
content.remove();
```

- 

## Event Handling

Events allow JavaScript to respond to user actions (e.g., clicks, keypresses). Use `addEventListener` to attach handlers:

```
const button = document.querySelector('button');

button.addEventListener('click', () => {

  alert('Button clicked!');

});
```

Common events:

- `click`: Mouse click.
- `input`: Form input changes.
- `mouseover`: Mouse hovers over an element.
- `keydown`: Key pressed.

Example: Toggle a class on click:

```
<button id="toggle">Toggle</button>

<div id="box">Box</div>

<script>

  const button = document.getElementById('toggle');

  const box = document.getElementById('box');

  button.addEventListener('click', () => {

    box.classList.toggle('active');

  });

</script>

<style>

  .active {

    background-color: yellow;

  }

</style>
```

## Event Delegation

Instead of attaching listeners to individual elements, use event delegation to handle events on a parent:

```
document.querySelector('ul').addEventListener('click', (e) => {

  if (e.target.tagName === 'LI') {

    e.target.style.color = 'red';

  }
```

```
});
```

This is efficient for dynamic lists where items are added or removed.

## Practical Applications

DOM manipulation enables:

**Form Validation**: Check input values before submission:

```
const form = document.querySelector('form');

form.addEventListener('submit', (e) => {

    e.preventDefault();

    const input = form.querySelector('input');

    if (input.value === '') {

        alert('Please fill in the field');

    }

});
```

-

**Dynamic Content**: Update content based on user actions or API data:

```
fetch('https://api.example.com/posts')

    .then(response => response.json())

    .then(data => {

        const list = document.querySelector('ul');

        data.forEach(item => {

            const li = document.createElement('li');

            li.textContent = item.title;
```

```
        list.appendChild(li);
    });
});
```

- 
- **Interactive UI**: Create toggles, modals, or sliders.

## Best Practices

**Minimize DOM Access**: Cache selectors in variables to improve performance:

```
const div = document.querySelector('div'); // Cache once
div.style.color = 'blue';
```

- 
- **Use Event Delegation**: For dynamic elements to reduce memory usage.
- **Ensure Accessibility**: Add ARIA attributes (e.g., `aria-live`) for dynamic updates.
- **Avoid Inline JavaScript**: Use `addEventListener` instead of `onclick`.
- **Test Performance**: Avoid excessive DOM manipulations in loops.

## Debugging

Use browser dev tools:

- **Console**: Log values with `console.log()` or `console.dir()` for DOM objects.
- **Elements Tab**: Inspect the DOM tree.
- **Sources Tab**: Set breakpoints to debug scripts.

# 4.4 Handling Events: Buttons, Forms, and User Actions

## The Importance of Event Handling

Event handling is the cornerstone of interactive web development, allowing JavaScript to respond to user actions such as clicks, form submissions, keyboard inputs, and mouse movements. By capturing and processing these events, developers can create dynamic, user-driven experiences, such as validating forms, updating content in real-time, or toggling UI elements. Understanding how to handle events effectively is essential for building responsive and engaging websites, making it a critical skill in JavaScript development.

## What Are Events?

Events are actions or occurrences in the browser, such as a user clicking a button, typing in a form, or scrolling a page. JavaScript listens for these events using event listeners, which trigger specific functions (event handlers) when an event occurs. The browser's event-driven model ensures that websites can respond instantly to user interactions, enhancing usability and engagement.

## Adding Event Listeners

The preferred method for handling events is the `addEventListener` method, which attaches a function to an element for a specific event type. The syntax is:

```
element.addEventListener('event', function(event) {

  // Handle the event

});
```

Common event types include:

- **click**: Triggered when an element is clicked.
- **submit**: Fired when a form is submitted.
- **input**: Occurs when a form input's value changes.

- **mouseover/mouseout**: Triggered when the mouse enters/leaves an element.
- **keydown/keyup**: Fired when a key is pressed/released.

Example: Handling a button click:

```
<button id="myButton">Click Me</button>

<script>

  const button = document.getElementById('myButton');

  button.addEventListener('click', () => {

    alert('Button clicked!');

  });

</script>
```

## Event Object

The event handler receives an `event` object containing details about the event, such as the target element, mouse coordinates, or key pressed. For example:

```
button.addEventListener('click', (event) => {

  console.log(event.target); // The clicked button

  console.log(event.type); // "click"

});
```

## Handling Form Events

Forms are a common source of user interaction, and JavaScript can enhance their functionality through event handling. Key form-related events include:

- **submit**: Triggered when a form is submitted (e.g., via a submit button).
- **input** or **change**: Fired when a form field's value changes.

Example: Validating a form submission:

```
<form id="myForm">
  <input type="text" id="username" required>
  <button type="submit">Submit</button>
</form>
<script>
  const form = document.getElementById('myForm');
  form.addEventListener('submit', (event) => {
    event.preventDefault(); // Prevent page reload
    const username = document.getElementById('username').value;
    if (username.length < 3) {
      alert('Username must be at least 3 characters.');
    } else {
      alert(`Welcome, ${username}!`);
    }
  });
</script>
```

The `event.preventDefault()` method stops the default form submission (e.g., page reload), allowing JavaScript to handle the logic.

## Event Delegation

For efficiency, especially with dynamic elements, use event delegation. Instead of attaching listeners to individual elements, attach one to a parent element and use the `event.target` to identify the triggered element:

```
<ul id="list">

  <li>Item 1</li>

  <li>Item 2</li>

</ul>

<script>

  const list = document.getElementById('list');

  list.addEventListener('click', (event) => {

    if (event.target.tagName === 'LI') {

      event.target.style.backgroundColor = 'yellow';

    }

  });

</script>
```

This approach is efficient for lists or elements added dynamically.

## Keyboard and Mouse Events

**Keyboard Events**: Use `keydown` or `keyup` to capture key presses:

```
document.addEventListener('keydown', (event) => {

  if (event.key === 'Enter') {

    console.log('Enter key pressed!');

  }
```

```
});
```

- 

**Mouse Events**: Use `mouseover`, `mouseout`, or `mousemove` for hover or drag effects:

```
const box = document.querySelector('.box');

box.addEventListener('mouseover', () => {

  box.style.backgroundColor = 'blue';

});

box.addEventListener('mouseout', () => {

  box.style.backgroundColor = '';

});
```

- 

## Event Bubbling and Capturing

Events propagate through the DOM in two phases:

- **Capturing**: From the document root to the target element.
- **Bubbling**: From the target element back to the root.

By default, `addEventListener` uses bubbling. To use capturing, set the third argument to `true`:

```
element.addEventListener('click', handler, true);
```

To stop propagation (e.g., prevent parent elements from handling the event):

```
event.stopPropagation();
```

## Accessibility Considerations

Ensure event handlers support accessibility:

- **Keyboard Accessibility**: Ensure interactive elements (e.g., buttons) are focusable via the `Tab` key and triggerable with `Enter` or `Space`.

**ARIA Attributes**: Use `aria-live` for dynamic updates or `aria-label` for clarity:
<button aria-label="Toggle menu">Menu</button>

- 
- **Avoid Mouse-Only Events**: Support equivalent keyboard events (e.g., `keydown` alongside `click`).

## Best Practices

- **Use `addEventListener`**: Avoid inline event handlers (e.g., `onclick="..."`) for maintainability.
- **Prevent Default Sparingly**: Only use `event.preventDefault()` when necessary (e.g., form submissions).

**Debounce/Throttle**: For frequent events like `scroll` or `resize`, use debouncing to limit execution:

```
function debounce(func, wait) {

  let timeout;

  return function() {

    clearTimeout(timeout);

    timeout = setTimeout(() => func.apply(this, arguments), wait);

  };

}

window.addEventListener('resize', debounce(() => console.log('Resized'), 200));
```

- 
- **Test Across Devices**: Ensure events work on touch devices and keyboards.

**Clean Up Listeners**: Remove unused listeners to prevent memory leaks:
button.removeEventListener('click', handler);

- 

## Practical Applications

- **Form Validation**: Check inputs in real-time or on submission.
- **Interactive Menus**: Toggle navigation menus on click.
- **Dynamic Content**: Update elements based on user actions (e.g., filtering a list).
- **Modals**: Show/hide dialog boxes on button clicks.

---

# 4.5 Introduction to Conditional Logic and Loops

## The Role of Logic in JavaScript

Conditional logic and loops are fundamental programming concepts that enable JavaScript to make decisions and perform repetitive tasks. Conditional logic allows code to execute different paths based on conditions, while loops repeat actions until a condition is met. These constructs are essential for creating dynamic, responsive web applications, such as validating user input, processing data, or iterating over elements. Understanding conditional logic and loops equips developers to write flexible, efficient code that responds to varying scenarios.

## Conditional Logic

Conditional statements control the flow of execution based on conditions, using `if`, `else if`, `else`, and `switch`.

### If Statements

The `if` statement executes code if a condition is true:

let age = 18;

if (age >= 18) {

```
    console.log('You are an adult.');
}
```

Add `else` for an alternative path:

```
if (age >= 18) {
    console.log('You are an adult.');
} else {
    console.log('You are a minor.');
}
```

Use `else if` for multiple conditions:

```
let score = 85;
if (score >= 90) {
    console.log('Grade: A');
} else if (score >= 80) {
    console.log('Grade: B');
} else {
    console.log('Grade: C or below');
}
```

**Comparison Operators**

Conditions use comparison operators:

- `===`: Strict equality (value and type).
- `!==`: Strict inequality.
- `>`, `<`, `>=`, `<=`: Greater than, less than, etc.
- `&&`: Logical AND (both conditions true).
- `||`: Logical OR (at least one condition true).
- `!`: Logical NOT.

Example:

```
let isLoggedIn = true;

let isAdmin = false;

if (isLoggedIn && !isAdmin) {

  console.log('Welcome, user!');

}
```

### Switch Statements

For multiple conditions based on a single value, use `switch`:

```
let day = 'Monday';

switch (day) {

  case 'Monday':

    console.log('Start of the week!');

    break;

  case 'Friday':

    console.log('Weekend is near!');

    break;

  default:
```

```
    console.log('Midweek day.');
}
```

The `break` statement prevents fall-through, and `default` handles unmatched cases.

**Ternary Operator**

For concise conditionals, use the ternary operator (`? :`):

```
let message = age >= 18 ? 'Adult' : 'Minor';
console.log(message); // "Adult"
```

## Loops

Loops repeat code until a condition is met, ideal for tasks like iterating over arrays or processing data.

**For Loop**

The `for` loop runs a set number of times:

```
for (let i = 0; i < 5; i++) {
  console.log(`Iteration ${i}`);
}
```

Structure: `for (initialization; condition; update)`.

**While Loop**

The `while` loop runs as long as a condition is true:

```
let count = 0;
while (count < 5) {
  console.log(`Count: ${count}`);
  count++;
}
```

**Do-While Loop**

The `do-while` loop runs at least once before checking the condition:

```
let i = 0;
do {
  console.log(`Do-while: ${i}`);
  i++;
} while (i < 5);
```

**For...Of Loop**

Iterates over iterable objects like arrays:

```
const numbers = [1, 2, 3];
for (let num of numbers) {
  console.log(num);
}
```

**For...In Loop**

Iterates over object properties:

```
const user = { name: 'Alice', age: 25 };

for (let key in user) {

  console.log(`${key}: ${user[key]}`);

}
```

### Breaking and Continuing

**break**: Exits the loop:

```
for (let i = 0; i < 10; i++) {

  if (i === 5) break;

  console.log(i);

}
```

- 

**continue**: Skips the current iteration:

```
for (let i = 0; i < 5; i++) {

  if (i === 3) continue;

  console.log(i);

}
```

- 

## Practical Applications

**Form Validation**: Use conditionals to check input values:

```
if (password.length < 8) {

  alert('Password too short');
```

```
}
```

- 

**Data Processing**: Use loops to iterate over arrays:

```
const scores = [85, 90, 78];

let total = 0;

for (let score of scores) {

  total += score;

}

console.log(`Average: ${total / scores.length}`);
```

- 

**Dynamic UI**: Update elements based on conditions or loops:

```
const list = document.querySelector('ul');

const items = ['Item 1', 'Item 2', 'Item 3'];

for (let item of items) {

  const li = document.createElement('li');

  li.textContent = item;

  list.appendChild(li);

}
```

- 

## Best Practices

- **Keep Conditions Clear**: Use descriptive variable names and simple logic.

**Avoid Infinite Loops**: Ensure loop conditions will eventually be false:

```
let i = 0;
```

```
while (i < 5) {

  console.log(i);

  i++; // Prevent infinite loop

}
```

- 
- **Use Appropriate Loops**: Choose `for` for known iterations, `while` for condition-based loops, and `for...of` for arrays.
- **Optimize Performance**: Avoid heavy operations inside loops.
- **Test Edge Cases**: Check conditions for null, undefined, or unexpected values.

---

# 4.6 Hands-On Project: Create a Simple Quiz App

### Project Overview

This hands-on project guides you through building a simple quiz application using HTML, CSS, and JavaScript. The quiz will display multiple-choice questions, track the user's score, and provide feedback. This project applies concepts from Chapter 4, including event handling, DOM manipulation, conditional logic, and loops, to create an interactive web application.

### Step 1: Setting Up the Project

Create a folder named `quiz-app` with the following structure:

```
quiz-app/

├── index.html

├── styles.css

├── script.js
```

Use Visual Studio Code and Live Server to preview the app.

## Step 2: Creating the HTML (`index.html`)

In `index.html`, add:

```
<!DOCTYPE html>
<html lang="en">
<head>
  <meta charset="UTF-8">
  <meta name="viewport" content="width=device-width, initial-scale=1.0">
  <title>Quiz App</title>
  <link rel="stylesheet" href="styles.css">
</head>
<body>
  <header>
    <h1>Quiz App</h1>
  </header>
  <main>
    <section id="quiz">
      <h2 id="question"></h2>
      <div id="options"></div>
      <button id="submit">Submit Answer</button>
    </section>
    <section id="result" class="hidden">
```

```
        <h2>Results</h2>
        <p id="score"></p>
        <button id="restart">Restart Quiz</button>
      </section>
    </main>
    <script src="script.js"></script>
</body>
</html>
```

This includes a header, a quiz section for questions and options, and a hidden results section.

## Step 3: Styling with CSS (`styles.css`)

In `styles.css`, add:

```
* {
    box-sizing: border-box;
    margin: 0;
    padding: 0;
}

body {
    font-family: Arial, sans-serif;
    background-color: #f4f4f4;
```

```
    padding: 20px;
}

header {
    text-align: center;
    background-color: #007bff;
    color: white;
    padding: 20px;
    margin-bottom: 20px;
    border-radius: 8px;
}

main {
    max-width: 600px;
    margin: 0 auto;
    background-color: white;
    padding: 20px;
    border-radius: 8px;
    box-shadow: 0 0 10px rgba(0, 0, 0, 0.1);
}

h2 {
```

```
    margin-bottom: 20px;
}

.option {
    display: block;
    padding: 10px;
    margin: 10px 0;
    background-color: #f0f0f0;
    border: 1px solid #ccc;
    border-radius: 5px;
    cursor: pointer;
}

.option:hover {
    background-color: #e0e0e0;
}

.option.selected {
    background-color: #007bff;
    color: white;
}
```

```
button {
    padding: 10px 20px;
    background-color: #007bff;
    color: white;
    border: none;
    border-radius: 5px;
    cursor: pointer;
}

button:hover {
    background-color: #0056b3;
}

.hidden {
    display: none;
}

@media (max-width: 600px) {
    main {
        padding: 15px;
    }
}
```

This CSS creates a clean, responsive design with styled buttons and options.

### Step 4: Adding JavaScript (`script.js`)

In `script.js`, add:

```
const quizData = [
  {
    question: "What is the capital of France?",
    options: ["Paris", "London", "Berlin", "Madrid"],
    answer: "Paris"
  },
  {
    question: "Which planet is known as the Red Planet?",
    options: ["Venus", "Mars", "Jupiter", "Saturn"],
    answer: "Mars"
  },
  {
    question: "What is 2 + 2?",
    options: ["3", "4", "5", "6"],
    answer: "4"
  }
];
```

```
let currentQuestion = 0;
let score = 0;

const questionEl = document.getElementById('question');
const optionsEl = document.getElementById('options');
const submitBtn = document.getElementById('submit');
const resultEl = document.getElementById('result');
const scoreEl = document.getElementById('score');
const restartBtn = document.getElementById('restart');

function loadQuestion() {
  const currentQuiz = quizData[currentQuestion];
  questionEl.textContent = currentQuiz.question;
  optionsEl.innerHTML = '';
  currentQuiz.options.forEach(option => {
    const div = document.createElement('div');
    div.classList.add('option');
    div.textContent = option;
    div.addEventListener('click', () => selectOption(div, option));
    optionsEl.appendChild(div);
  });
}
```

```
function selectOption(div, option) {
    const options = optionsEl.querySelectorAll('.option');
    options.forEach(opt => opt.classList.remove('selected'));
    div.classList.add('selected');
    submitBtn.disabled = false;
}

submitBtn.addEventListener('click', () => {
    const selectedOption = optionsEl.querySelector('.selected');
    if (selectedOption && selectedOption.textContent ===
quizData[currentQuestion].answer) {
        score++;
    }
    currentQuestion++;
    if (currentQuestion < quizData.length) {
        loadQuestion();
        submitBtn.disabled = true;
    } else {
        showResult();
    }
});
```

```
restartBtn.addEventListener('click', () => {
    currentQuestion = 0;
    score = 0;
    resultEl.classList.add('hidden');
    quizEl.classList.remove('hidden');
    submitBtn.disabled = true;
    loadQuestion();
});

function showResult() {
    quizEl.classList.add('hidden');
    resultEl.classList.remove('hidden');
    scoreEl.textContent = `You scored ${score} out of ${quizData.length}!`;
}

// Initialize
loadQuestion();
submitBtn.disabled = true;
```

This JavaScript:

- Defines a `quizData` array with questions, options, and answers.

- Tracks the current question and score.
- Loads questions and options dynamically using DOM manipulation.
- Handles option selection and submission with event listeners.
- Uses conditional logic to check answers and loops to iterate over options.
- Shows results and allows restarting the quiz.

## Step 5: Testing and Validation

- Open `index.html` with Live Server to test the quiz functionality.
- Verify that questions load, options are selectable, scores are tracked, and the restart button works.
- Test responsiveness on mobile devices using DevTools.
- Check accessibility with WAVE or Lighthouse, ensuring keyboard navigation and ARIA support.
- Debug with `console.log()` if issues arise.

## Step 6: Enhancements

To extend the project:

- Add feedback for correct/incorrect answers.
- Include a timer for each question.
- Store scores in `localStorage` for persistence.
- Deploy to GitHub Pages.

# Chapter 5

# Best Practices in Web Development

## 5.1 Writing Clean and Accessible HTML

### The Importance of Clean and Accessible HTML

HTML serves as the backbone of every webpage, defining its structure and content. Writing clean and accessible HTML is crucial for creating websites that are maintainable, scalable, and usable by all users, including those with disabilities. Clean HTML is well-organized, easy to read, and follows standardized conventions, making it simpler for developers to collaborate and maintain codebases. Accessible HTML ensures that websites are usable by people with visual, auditory, motor, or cognitive impairments, aligning with ethical and legal standards like the Web Content Accessibility Guidelines (WCAG). By adhering to best practices in writing clean and accessible HTML, developers can create robust, inclusive websites that enhance user experience and improve search engine optimization (SEO).

### Characteristics of Clean HTML

Clean HTML is structured, readable, and free of unnecessary complexity. Key characteristics include:

- **Semantic Structure**: Using meaningful elements like `<header>`, `<nav>`, `<main>`, `<article>`, and `<footer>` instead of generic `<div>` tags. Semantic HTML conveys the purpose of content, improving readability for developers and machines.
- **Minimal Markup**: Avoiding excessive nesting or redundant elements. For example, instead of wrapping every element in a `<div>`, use semantic elements or CSS for layout.
- **Consistent Formatting**: Using consistent indentation (e.g., two spaces) and lowercase tags for readability. Tools like Prettier can automate formatting.

**Commented Code**: Adding comments to explain complex sections:
<!-- Navigation menu -->

```
<nav>

  <ul>

    <li><a href="index.html">Home</a></li>

  </ul>

</nav>
```

- 
- **Valid Code**: Ensuring HTML adheres to W3C standards, validated using tools like the W3C Markup Validator.

Example of clean HTML:

```
<!DOCTYPE html>

<html lang="en">

<head>

  <meta charset="UTF-8">

  <meta name="viewport" content="width=device-width, initial-scale=1.0">

  <title>My Website</title>

  <link rel="stylesheet" href="styles.css">

</head>

<body>

  <header>

    <h1>Welcome to My Website</h1>

    <nav>

      <ul>

        <li><a href="#home">Home</a></li>
```

```
            <li><a href="#about">About</a></li>
        </ul>
    </nav>
  </header>
  <main>
    <section id="about">
        <h2>About Us</h2>
        <p>We are passionate about creating accessible websites.</p>
    </section>
  </main>
  <footer>
    <p>&copy; 2025 My Website</p>
  </footer>
</body>
</html>
```

## Accessibility in HTML

Accessibility ensures that websites are usable by everyone, including those using assistive technologies like screen readers. Key practices include:

- **Semantic Elements**: Use elements like `<nav>`, `<main>`, and `<article>` to provide context. For example, `<nav>` indicates a navigation section, helping screen readers identify it.

**ARIA Attributes**: Add Accessible Rich Internet Applications (ARIA) attributes to enhance accessibility:

```
<button aria-label="Close menu">X</button>
```

- Use role to define element purposes (e.g., <div role="alert">).

**Alt Text for Images**: Provide descriptive alt attributes for <img> tags:

```
<img src="photo.jpg" alt="A sunset over the mountains">
```

-
- **Keyboard Navigation**: Ensure all interactive elements (e.g., buttons, links) are focusable via the Tab key and triggerable with Enter or Space.
- **Proper Heading Structure**: Use <h1> to <h6> in a logical hierarchy (e.g., one <h1> per page, followed by <h2>, <h3>, etc.).

**Form Accessibility**: Use <label> with for attributes and aria-describedby for error messages:

```
<label for="username">Username:</label>

<input id="username" type="text" aria-describedby="error">

<span id="error" class="hidden">Username is required.</span>
```

-

## Best Practices for Clean and Accessible HTML

- **Use Semantic HTML**: Replace <div class="header"> with <header> for clarity and accessibility.
- **Keep It Simple**: Avoid unnecessary elements or inline styles (e.g., <p style="color: blue;">). Use external CSS instead.
- **Validate Regularly**: Use the W3C Markup Validator to catch errors like unclosed tags or missing attributes.
- **Test with Assistive Technologies**: Use screen readers (e.g., NVDA, VoiceOver) to verify accessibility.
- **Maintain Language Attributes**: Include lang="en" in the <html> tag to assist screen readers.
- **Avoid Deprecated Elements**: Steer clear of outdated tags like <font> or <center>; use CSS instead.

- **Document Structure**: Ensure every page has a `<!DOCTYPE html>` declaration and a `<meta charset="UTF-8">` for proper rendering.

## Benefits of Clean and Accessible HTML

- **Maintainability**: Clean code is easier to update and debug, especially in collaborative projects.
- **Accessibility Compliance**: Adhering to WCAG ensures inclusivity and may be legally required in some regions.
- **SEO**: Semantic HTML improves search engine indexing, as crawlers understand content better.
- **User Experience**: Accessible websites provide a consistent experience for all users, including those with disabilities.
- **Future-Proofing**: Clean, standards-compliant HTML is more compatible with new browsers and technologies.

## Tools for Writing Clean and Accessible HTML

- **Linters**: Tools like HTMLHint or VS Code extensions catch syntax errors.
- **Accessibility Checkers**: WAVE, axe, or Lighthouse evaluate accessibility compliance.
- **Code Formatters**: Prettier or Beautify ensure consistent formatting.
- **Screen Readers**: Test with NVDA (Windows), VoiceOver (macOS), or TalkBack (Android).

## Practical Example

Consider a form with accessibility features:

```
<form id="contact-form">

  <div>

    <label for="name">Name:</label>

    <input id="name" type="text" required aria-required="true">

  </div>

  <div>
```

```
    <label for="message">Message:</label>

    <textarea id="message" aria-describedby="message-error"></textarea>

    <span id="message-error" class="hidden">Please enter a message.</span>

  </div>

  <button type="submit">Send</button>

</form>
```

This form uses semantic elements, labels, and ARIA attributes for accessibility, with clean structure for maintainability.

## Challenges and Solutions

- **Challenge**: Overuse of `<div>` leading to "div soup."
  - **Solution**: Use semantic elements and plan the structure before coding.
- **Challenge**: Missing alt text or inaccessible forms.
  - **Solution**: Always include `alt` attributes and test forms with keyboard navigation.
- **Challenge**: Inconsistent formatting across teams.
  - **Solution**: Adopt a style guide (e.g., Google HTML/CSS Style Guide) and use linters.

---

# 5.2 Optimizing CSS for Performance and Reusability

## The Importance of Optimized CSS

CSS is critical for styling webpages, but poorly written or inefficient CSS can slow down page rendering, increase load times, and complicate maintenance. Optimizing CSS for performance ensures fast, responsive websites, while designing for reusability reduces code duplication and simplifies updates. As websites grow in complexity, efficient and reusable CSS becomes essential for delivering seamless user experiences across devices and maintaining scalable codebases. This section explores best practices for optimizing CSS performance and creating reusable styles, ensuring websites are both fast and maintainable.

## CSS Performance Optimization

Performance optimization focuses on reducing CSS file size, minimizing rendering delays, and improving browser efficiency. Key strategies include:

### Minification and Compression

**Minification**: Remove unnecessary characters (e.g., whitespace, comments) to reduce file size. Tools like CSSNano or UglifyCSS automate this:

```
/* Before */

.container {

   margin: 20px;

   padding: 10px;

}



/* After */

.container{margin:20px;padding:10px}
```

-

- **Compression**: Use Gzip or Brotli on the server to compress CSS files before transmission, reducing download time.

**Reducing CSS Selectors**

**Avoid Overly Specific Selectors**: Complex selectors like `div ul li a` are slower to process than simple ones like `.nav-link`. Use class-based selectors for efficiency:

```
.nav-link {

  color: #007bff;

}
```

- 

**Limit Universal Selectors**: The `*` selector is resource-intensive. Scope styles to specific elements:

```
.container * {

  box-sizing: border-box; /* Less efficient */

}

main {

  box-sizing: border-box; /* More efficient */

}
```

- 

**Critical CSS**

Extract and inline critical CSS (styles needed for above-the-fold content) in the `<head>` to speed up initial rendering:

```
<style>

  header {

    background-color: #007bff;
```

```
    color: white;
  }
</style>
```

Use tools like Critical to automate this process, deferring non-critical CSS with `async` or `defer` attributes.

### Avoiding Expensive Properties

Some CSS properties, like `box-shadow`, `border-radius`, or `filter`, are computationally expensive. Use them judiciously and test performance with browser dev tools' Performance tab.

### Leveraging Browser Caching

Use cache-control headers to cache CSS files, reducing server requests for returning users. Example server configuration (Apache):

```
<FilesMatch "\.css$">
  Header set Cache-Control "max-age=31536000, public"
</FilesMatch>
```

### Responsive Design with Media Queries

Use media queries efficiently to avoid redundant styles:

```
@media (max-width: 600px) {
  .container {
    padding: 10px;
  }
}
```

Combine related media queries and avoid duplicating rules across breakpoints.

## Designing for Reusability

Reusable CSS reduces code duplication, simplifies maintenance, and ensures consistency. Key techniques include:

### CSS Variables

Custom properties (variables) allow reusable values:

```
:root {
    --primary-color: #007bff;
    --padding: 20px;
}
button {
    background-color: var(--primary-color);
    padding: var(--padding);
}
```

Update variables in one place to affect the entire site.

### Modular CSS with BEM

The Block Element Modifier (BEM) methodology organizes classes for reusability:

```
.button {
    padding: 10px;
}
```

```
.button--primary {
    background-color: var(--primary-color);
}
.button__text {
    font-weight: bold;
}

<button class="button button--primary">
    <span class="button__text">Click Me</span>
</button>
```

BEM ensures clear, reusable class names.

**Utility-First CSS**

Frameworks like Tailwind CSS use utility classes for reusability:

```
<div class="bg-blue-500 text-white p-4 rounded">
    Content
</div>
```

Utility classes reduce custom CSS and speed up development.

**Component-Based Styling**

Create reusable components for common UI elements (e.g., buttons, cards):

```
.card {
```

```
    border: 1px solid #ccc;
    border-radius: 8px;
    padding: 20px;
}
.card--featured {
    border-color: var(--primary-color);
}
```

Apply components across pages for consistency.

**Normalize or Reset CSS**

Use a CSS reset (e.g., `normalize.css`) to standardize browser defaults:

```
* {
    margin: 0;
    padding: 0;
    box-sizing: border-box;
}
```

This ensures consistent styling across browsers.

## Best Practices

**Organize Stylesheets**: Group styles by component or section with comments:

```
/* Header Styles */
header { ... }
```

```
/* Main Content */

main { ... }
```

- 

**Use CSS Preprocessors**: Tools like Sass or Less enable variables, nesting, and mixins for reusable code:

```
$primary: #007bff;

.button {

   padding: 10px;

   &.primary {

      background-color: $primary;

   }

}
```

- 
- **Test Performance**: Use Lighthouse or PageSpeed Insights to identify CSS bottlenecks.
- **Maintain Accessibility**: Ensure styles support accessibility (e.g., sufficient contrast, readable fonts).
- **Version Control**: Use Git to track CSS changes and collaborate effectively.

## Practical Example

A reusable, optimized card component:

```
:root {

   --card-border: 1px solid #ccc;

   --card-padding: 20px;

}
```

```
.card {
    border: var(--card-border);
    border-radius: 8px;
    padding: var(--card-padding);
    background-color: white;
    box-shadow: 0 2px 4px rgba(0, 0, 0, 0.1);
}

.card--featured {
    border-color: var(--primary-color);
}

@media (max-width: 600px) {
    .card {
        padding: 15px;
    }
}

<div class="card">
    <h2>Card Title</h2>
    <p>Content here.</p>
</div>
```

This uses variables, modular classes, and media queries for performance and reusability.

### Challenges and Solutions

- **Challenge**: Large CSS files slowing down load times.
    - **Solution**: Minify, compress, and use critical CSS.
- **Challenge**: Inconsistent styling across pages.
    - **Solution**: Use variables and component-based styling.
- **Challenge**: Browser compatibility issues.
    - **Solution**: Test with tools like BrowserStack and use vendor prefixes (e.g., `-webkit-`) when needed.

## 5.3 Debugging JavaScript: Common Errors and Fixes

### The Importance of Debugging JavaScript

JavaScript is the engine behind interactive web applications, but its dynamic nature makes it prone to errors that can disrupt functionality or degrade user experience. Debugging is the process of identifying, diagnosing, and fixing these errors to ensure code runs smoothly. Effective debugging saves time, improves code quality, and enhances website reliability. By mastering debugging techniques and understanding common JavaScript errors, developers can create robust applications, streamline development, and maintain user trust. This section explores the debugging process, common JavaScript errors, and tools and strategies to resolve them efficiently.

### The Debugging Process

Debugging involves three key steps:

1. **Identify the Error**: Recognize symptoms, such as broken functionality, unexpected behavior, or console errors.
2. **Diagnose the Cause**: Use tools to trace the error's origin, such as incorrect logic, syntax issues, or DOM manipulation errors.
3. **Fix the Issue**: Apply targeted solutions and test to ensure the fix works without introducing new problems.

## Common JavaScript Errors

JavaScript errors fall into several categories, each with distinct causes and fixes:

### 1. Syntax Errors

Syntax errors occur when code violates JavaScript's grammatical rules, preventing execution. Common examples:

- **Missing Semicolons**: `let x = 5` (missing `;` can cause issues in some contexts).
- **Unclosed Brackets/Parentheses**: `function example() { console.log("Test")` (missing `}`).
- **Fix**: Use a linter (e.g., ESLint) to catch syntax issues and check the browser console for errors like `SyntaxError: Unexpected token`.

Example:

```
function greet() {
  console.log("Hello" // Missing parenthesis and semicolon
}
```

**Fix**:

```
function greet() {
  console.log("Hello");
}
```

### 2. Reference Errors

Reference errors occur when accessing undefined variables or functions:

- **Cause**: Using a variable before declaration (e.g., `console.log(x);` before `let x = 5;`).

- **Fix**: Ensure variables are declared before use and check scope:

```
let x = 5;

console.log(x); // Works
```

### 3. Type Errors

Type errors happen when an operation is performed on an incompatible data type:

- **Cause**: Accessing properties on `undefined` or `null` (e.g., `null.toString()`).
- **Fix**: Check for `undefined` or `null` before operations:

```
let obj = null;

if (obj) {

   console.log(obj.toString());

} else {

   console.log("Object is null");

}
```

### 4. DOM-Related Errors

Errors during DOM manipulation are common, especially when elements are not found:

- **Cause**: Selecting non-existent elements (e.g., `document.getElementById('missing')` returns `null`).
- **Fix**: Verify element existence before manipulation:

```
const element = document.getElementById('myElement');

if (element) {
```

```
    element.style.color = 'blue';
} else {
    console.error('Element not found');
}
```

**5. Asynchronous Errors**

Asynchronous operations, like `fetch`, can fail due to network issues or incorrect handling:

- **Cause**: Not handling promise rejections (e.g., `fetch('invalid-url')`).
- **Fix**: Use `try/catch` with async/await or `.catch()` with promises:

```
async function getData() {
    try {
        const response = await fetch('https://api.example.com/data');
        const data = await response.json();
        console.log(data);
    } catch (error) {
        console.error('Fetch error:', error);
    }
}
```

## Debugging Tools

Modern browsers and development environments offer powerful debugging tools:

- **Browser Developer Tools**:
  - **Console**: Displays errors, warnings, and `console.log()` output. Use `console.error()`, `console.warn()`, or `console.dir()` for detailed debugging.
  - **Sources Tab**: Set breakpoints to pause execution and inspect variables.
  - **Network Tab**: Monitor network requests (e.g., failed API calls).

**Linters**: ESLint catches syntax errors, unused variables, and style issues. Configure in VS Code with:

```
{
  "eslint.validate": ["javascript"]
}
```

- 

**Debuggers**: Use the `debugger` statement to pause execution:

```
function calculateTotal(price) {
  debugger; // Pauses execution
  return price * 1.1;
}
```

- 
- **Online Tools**: Platforms like JSFiddle or CodePen allow testing and debugging in isolated environments.

## Debugging Strategies

- **Reproduce the Issue**: Consistently trigger the error to understand its context.

**Use Console Logging**: Add `console.log()` to track variable values and program flow:

```
function processArray(arr) {
  console.log('Input array:', arr);
```

```
    return arr.map(item => item * 2);

}
```

- 
- **Break Down Code**: Test small sections to isolate the error.
- **Check Browser Compatibility**: Use Can I Use to verify feature support and test across Chrome, Firefox, Safari, and Edge.
- **Handle Edge Cases**: Test for `null`, `undefined`, empty inputs, or unexpected data types.
- **Version Control**: Use Git to revert to a working state if debugging introduces issues.

## Best Practices

**Write Defensive Code**: Check for errors before operations:

```
if (typeof data === 'object' && data !== null) {

    console.log(data.name);

}
```

- 

**Use Strict Mode**: Enable `"use strict";` to catch undeclared variables:

```
"use strict";

x = 5; // ReferenceError
```

- 
- **Modularize Code**: Break code into small, testable functions to simplify debugging.
- **Test Incrementally**: Add and test features one at a time to catch errors early.
- **Document Errors**: Log common issues and fixes in project documentation.

## Practical Example

Debugging a form validation issue:

```
<form id="form">
```

```
  <input id="email" type="email">
  <button type="submit">Submit</button>
</form>
<script>
  const form = document.getElementById('form');
  form.addEventListener('submit', (e) => {
    e.preventDefault();
    const email = document.getElementById('email').value;
    console.log('Email:', email); // Debug input
    if (!email.includes('@')) {
      console.error('Invalid email'); // Log error
      alert('Please enter a valid email.');
    } else {
      console.log('Form submitted'); // Confirm success
      alert('Form submitted!');
    }
  });
</script>
```

This code logs inputs and errors to the console, making it easier to diagnose issues.

## Challenges and Solutions

- **Challenge**: Silent errors (no console output).

    - **Solution**: Add `console.log()` or use breakpoints to trace execution.
- **Challenge**: Asynchronous bugs (e.g., race conditions).
    - **Solution**: Use `async/await` or `.catch()` and log promise states.
- **Challenge**: Browser-specific issues.
    - **Solution**: Test with multiple browsers and use polyfills for unsupported features.

---

# 5.4 Ensuring Website Accessibility for All Users

## The Importance of Web Accessibility

Web accessibility ensures that websites are usable by everyone, including people with disabilities such as visual, auditory, motor, or cognitive impairments. Accessible websites align with ethical principles, legal requirements (e.g., WCAG, ADA), and business goals by reaching a broader audience. Accessibility enhances user experience, improves SEO, and fosters inclusivity, making it a cornerstone of modern web development. By prioritizing accessibility, developers create websites that are equitable, compliant, and user-friendly, ensuring no one is excluded from digital experiences.

## Understanding Accessibility Standards

The Web Content Accessibility Guidelines (WCAG) provide a framework for accessibility, organized around four principles (POUR):

- **Perceivable**: Content must be presented in ways users can perceive (e.g., text alternatives for images).
- **Operable**: Interfaces must be navigable and usable (e.g., keyboard accessibility).
- **Understandable**: Content and navigation must be clear and predictable.
- **Robust**: Content must be compatible with assistive technologies and future browsers.

WCAG levels (A, AA, AAA) define compliance, with Level AA being the common target for most websites.

## Key Accessibility Practices

### 1. Semantic HTML

Use semantic elements to provide context:

- <header>, <nav>, <main>, <footer> for structure.
- <h1> to <h6> for logical heading hierarchies.
- <button> and <a> for interactive elements, avoiding <div onclick="...">.

Example:

```
<nav aria-label="Main navigation">

  <ul>

    <li><a href="index.html" aria-current="page">Home</a></li>

    <li><a href="about.html">About</a></li>

  </ul>

</nav>
```

### 2. ARIA Attributes

Accessible Rich Internet Applications (ARIA) attributes enhance dynamic content:

- aria-label: Describes elements (e.g., <button aria-label="Close menu">X</button>).
- aria-live: Announces dynamic updates (e.g., <div aria-live="polite">Updated</div>).
- role: Defines element purpose (e.g., <div role="alert">Error</div>).

Example:

```
<div role="dialog" aria-labelledby="dialog-title">
```

```
    <h2 id="dialog-title">Confirm Action</h2>

</div>
```

### 3. Keyboard Navigation

Ensure all interactive elements are accessible via keyboard:

- Use `Tab` to navigate, `Enter` or `Space` to activate.
- Maintain a logical tab order with `tabindex`.

Provide visible focus indicators:

```
a:focus, button:focus {

    outline: 2px solid #007bff;

}
```

-

### 4. Text Alternatives

Provide alternatives for non-text content:

**Images**: Use descriptive `alt` attributes:

```
<img src="photo.jpg" alt="A dog playing in a park">
```

-

**Videos/Audio**: Include captions or transcripts:

```
<video controls>

    <source src="video.mp4" type="video/mp4">

    <track src="captions.vtt" kind="subtitles" srclang="en" label="English">

</video>
```

-

### 5. Color and Contrast

Ensure sufficient contrast for readability (WCAG 4.5:1 for normal text):

- Use tools like WebAIM's Contrast Checker.

Avoid relying solely on color for meaning:

```
.error {

  border: 2px solid red;

  background-color: #ffe6e6; /* Not just color */

}
```

### 6. Forms

Make forms accessible:

Use `<label>` with `for` attributes:

```
<label for="email">Email:</label>

<input id="email" type="email" required>
```

Provide error feedback with `aria-describedby`:

```
<input id="email" aria-describedby="email-error">

<span id="email-error" class="hidden">Invalid email.</span>
```

## Testing for Accessibility

- **Manual Testing**: Use screen readers (NVDA, VoiceOver) to verify navigation and content.
- **Automated Tools**: Run WAVE, axe, or Lighthouse to identify issues.
- **Keyboard Testing**: Navigate the site using only the keyboard.
- **User Testing**: Involve users with disabilities to provide real-world feedback.

## Best Practices

- **Plan for Accessibility Early**: Integrate accessibility into the design phase.
- **Use Semantic HTML**: Avoid non-semantic elements for interactive features.
- **Test Across Devices**: Ensure accessibility on mobile and desktop.
- **Document Accessibility**: Include an accessibility statement on the website.
- **Stay Updated**: Follow WCAG updates and emerging accessibility standards.

## Practical Example

An accessible form:

```
<form id="signup">

  <div>

    <label for="username">Username:</label>

    <input id="username" type="text" required aria-required="true"
aria-describedby="username-error">

    <span id="username-error" class="hidden">Username must be at least 3
characters.</span>

  </div>

  <button type="submit" aria-label="Submit signup form">Sign Up</button>

</form>

<script>

  const form = document.getElementById('signup');

  form.addEventListener('submit', (e) => {

    e.preventDefault();

    const username = document.getElementById('username').value;

    const error = document.getElementById('username-error');

    if (username.length < 3) {

      error.classList.remove('hidden');
```

```
        error.setAttribute('aria-live', 'assertive');
      } else {
        error.classList.add('hidden');
        alert('Form submitted!');
      }
    });
</script>
<style>
  .hidden {
    display: none;
  }
</style>
```

This form is accessible with labels, ARIA attributes, and keyboard support.

## Challenges and Solutions

- **Challenge**: Retrofitting accessibility is time-consuming.
  - **Solution**: Build accessibility into the initial design and development process.
- **Challenge**: Ensuring screen reader compatibility.
  - **Solution**: Test with multiple screen readers and use ARIA sparingly to enhance, not replace, semantic HTML.
- **Challenge**: Maintaining accessibility in dynamic content.
  - **Solution**: Use `aria-live` and test dynamic updates thoroughly.

---

# 5.5 Testing Your Website Across Browsers

## The Need for Cross-Browser Testing

Cross-browser testing ensures that websites function and appear consistently across different browsers (e.g., Chrome, Firefox, Safari, Edge) and devices. Each browser has its own rendering engine (e.g., Blink for Chrome, Gecko for Firefox, WebKit for Safari), leading to variations in how HTML, CSS, and JavaScript are interpreted. Inconsistent rendering or functionality can frustrate users and harm a website's reputation. By testing across browsers, developers identify and fix compatibility issues, ensuring a seamless experience for all users. This section covers the importance, tools, and strategies for effective cross-browser testing.

## Why Cross-Browser Testing Matters

- **User Diversity**: Users access websites on various browsers, versions, and devices (e.g., desktops, mobiles, tablets).
- **Rendering Differences**: Browsers interpret CSS and JavaScript differently, causing layout or functionality issues.
- **Feature Support**: Not all browsers support the same features (e.g., CSS Grid or ES6+ JavaScript).
- **Performance Variations**: Load times and performance can differ across browsers.
- **SEO and Accessibility**: Consistent rendering supports search engine indexing and accessibility compliance.

## Common Cross-Browser Issues

- **CSS Differences**:
  - Vendor prefixes needed for some properties (e.g., `-webkit-transition` for Safari).
  - Inconsistent box model or flexbox behavior.
- **JavaScript Compatibility**:
  - Unsupported ES6+ features in older browsers (e.g., arrow functions in IE11).
  - Event handling differences (e.g., `event.preventDefault()` in older browsers).
- **HTML Parsing**: Variations in handling invalid HTML or deprecated tags.

- **Performance**: Slower rendering in resource-constrained browsers or devices.

## Tools for Cross-Browser Testing

- **Browser Developer Tools**: Chrome DevTools, Firefox Developer Tools, and Safari Web Inspector allow testing and debugging.
- **Cross-Browser Testing Platforms**:
  - **BrowserStack**: Test on real browsers and devices in the cloud.
  - **Sauce Labs**: Similar to BrowserStack, with automation support.
  - **LambdaTest**: Offers live and automated testing across browsers.
- **Virtual Machines**: Run different browser versions locally (e.g., VirtualBox with Windows for Edge testing).
- **Can I Use**: Check feature support across browsers (e.g., caniuse.com for CSS Grid).
- **Lighthouse**: Audit performance, accessibility, and SEO in Chrome DevTools.

## Testing Strategies

### 1. Manual Testing

Manually test key features (e.g., navigation, forms, interactivity) in target browsers:

- **Browsers**: Chrome, Firefox, Safari, Edge, and older versions like IE11 if needed.
- **Devices**: Desktops, tablets, and mobiles (use DevTools' device emulation).
- **Operating Systems**: Windows, macOS, Linux, iOS, Android.

### 2. Automated Testing

Use tools to automate repetitive tests:

**Selenium**: Automates browser interactions:

```
const { Builder, By } = require('selenium-webdriver');

async function test() {

  let driver = await new Builder().forBrowser('chrome').build();

  await driver.get('https://example.com');
```

```
    let title = await driver.findElement(By.tagName('h1')).getText();

    console.log(title);

    await driver.quit();

}
```

- 
- **Cypress**: End-to-end testing for modern web apps.
- **Playwright**: Cross-browser testing with a simple API.

**3. Responsive Testing**

Test layouts across screen sizes using:

**Media Queries**: Verify responsiveness:

```
@media (max-width: 600px) {

    .container {

        flex-direction: column;

    }

}
```

- 
- **DevTools Device Mode**: Emulate mobile devices in Chrome or Firefox.
- **Real Devices**: Test on physical devices for accurate touch and performance results.

**4. Feature Detection**

Use tools like Modernizr to detect feature support and provide fallbacks:

```
<script src="modernizr.js"></script>

<script>

    if (Modernizr.flexbox) {

        // Use Flexbox
```

```
    } else {

        // Fallback to floats

    }

</script>
```

**5. Polyfills**

Add polyfills for unsupported features:

**CSS**: Use `autoprefixer` to add vendor prefixes:

```
.box {

    transition: all 0.3s; /* Autoprefixer adds -webkit- for Safari */

}
```

- 
- **JavaScript**: Use polyfills for ES6+ features (e.g., `core-js` for `Promise`).

## Best Practices

- **Define Target Browsers**: Focus on popular browsers (e.g., latest Chrome, Firefox, Safari, Edge) based on user analytics.
- **Use a CSS Reset**: Normalize styles with `normalize.css` to reduce inconsistencies.
- **Test Early and Often**: Test during development, not just at the end.
- **Automate Where Possible**: Use CI/CD pipelines (e.g., GitHub Actions) to run automated tests.
- **Document Issues**: Log browser-specific bugs and fixes in project documentation.

## Practical Example

Test a button's functionality across browsers:

```
<button id="action">Click Me</button>
```

```
<script>
  document.getElementById('action').addEventListener('click', () => {
    document.body.style.backgroundColor = 'lightblue';
  });
</script>
<style>
  button {
    padding: 10px;
    background-color: #007bff;
    color: white;
    border-radius: 5px;
    transition: background-color 0.3s;
  }
  button:hover {
    background-color: #0056b3;
  }
</style>
```

- **Test**: Check if the click event works, the hover effect renders, and the transition is smooth in Chrome, Firefox, Safari, and Edge.
- **Issues**: Safari may require `-webkit-transition`. Older browsers may not support arrow functions.
- **Fix**: Add prefixes with Autoprefixer and transpile JavaScript with Babel.

## Challenges and Solutions

- **Challenge**: Inconsistent CSS rendering.
  - **Solution**: Use vendor prefixes and test with BrowserStack.
- **Challenge**: JavaScript feature support.
  - **Solution**: Use polyfills and feature detection.
- **Challenge**: Resource constraints for testing all browsers.
  - **Solution**: Prioritize popular browsers and use cloud testing platforms.

# Chapter 6

# Bringing It All Together

## 6.1 Combining HTML, CSS, and JavaScript

### The Synergy of HTML, CSS, and JavaScript

The creation of modern, interactive websites relies on the seamless integration of HTML, CSS, and JavaScript, each serving a distinct yet complementary role. HTML provides the structure, defining the content and layout of a webpage; CSS enhances the visual presentation, ensuring an aesthetically pleasing and responsive design; and JavaScript adds interactivity, enabling dynamic behavior and real-time updates. When combined effectively, these technologies produce engaging, user-friendly websites that meet the demands of today's digital landscape. This section explores how to integrate HTML, CSS, and JavaScript, highlighting best practices, practical examples, and strategies for creating cohesive web experiences.

### Roles of Each Technology

- **HTML (Structure)**: HTML forms the backbone of a webpage, using semantic elements like `<header>`, `<main>`, `<nav>`, and `<footer>` to organize content. It defines what appears on the page, such as text, images, and forms, and provides the foundation for styling and scripting.
- **CSS (Presentation)**: CSS controls the visual appearance, including colors, fonts, layouts, and animations. It uses selectors to target HTML elements and apply styles, ensuring consistency across pages and responsiveness across devices.
- **JavaScript (Behavior)**: JavaScript adds interactivity, manipulating the Document Object Model (DOM) to update content, handle user events (e.g., clicks, form submissions), and fetch data from APIs. It enables features like dynamic forms, modals, and real-time updates.

Together, these technologies create a complete web experience: HTML structures a form, CSS styles it, and JavaScript validates user input or submits data.

## Integrating HTML, CSS, and JavaScript

To combine these technologies, developers typically follow a modular approach, keeping each component separate for maintainability:

- **HTML**: Create a semantic structure in an `.html` file.

**CSS**: Store styles in an external `.css` file, linked via `<link>`:

```
<link rel="stylesheet" href="styles.css">
```

-

**JavaScript**: Write scripts in a `.js` file, linked via `<script>`:

```
<script src="script.js"></script>
```

-

This separation ensures clean code and simplifies updates. For example, a button can be structured, styled, and made interactive:

```
<!-- index.html -->

<button id="toggle">Toggle Theme</button>



/* styles.css */

button {

  padding: 10px 20px;

  background-color: #007bff;

  color: white;

  border: none;

  border-radius: 5px;

  cursor: pointer;
```

```
}

button:hover {
    background-color: #0056b3;
}


// script.js
const button = document.getElementById('toggle');
button.addEventListener('click', () => {
    document.body.classList.toggle('dark');
});


/* styles.css */
.dark {
    background-color: #333;
    color: white;
}
```

This example demonstrates HTML providing structure, CSS styling the button and theme, and JavaScript toggling a dark mode.

## Best Practices for Integration

**Semantic HTML**: Use elements like `<nav>` and `<article>` to provide context for CSS and JavaScript:

```
<nav aria-label="Main navigation">
```

```
    <ul>

        <li><a href="index.html" class="nav-link">Home</a></li>

    </ul>

</nav>
```

- 

**Modular CSS**: Use classes and CSS variables for reusability:

```
:root {

    --primary: #007bff;

}

.nav-link {

    color: var(--primary);

}
```

- 

**Event-Driven JavaScript**: Use `addEventListener` for clean event handling:

```
document.querySelector('.nav-link').addEventListener('click', (e) => {

    e.preventDefault();

    console.log('Link clicked');

});
```

- 
- **Separation of Concerns**: Avoid inline styles (`<p style="color: blue;">`) or inline JavaScript (`<button onclick="myFunction()">`). Use external files to keep code organized.

**Progressive Enhancement**: Ensure the site is functional without JavaScript (e.g., forms submit to a server) and enhance with JavaScript for better experiences:

```
<form action="/submit" method="post">
```

```
  <input type="text" name="username">
  <button type="submit">Submit</button>
</form>
<script>
  const form = document.querySelector('form');
  form.addEventListener('submit', async (e) => {
    e.preventDefault();
    // Handle form submission via JavaScript
  });
</script>
```

- 

## Practical Example: Interactive Form

Consider a contact form that validates input and provides feedback:

```
<!-- index.html -->
<form id="contact-form">
  <label for="name">Name:</label>
  <input id="name" type="text" required>
  <span id="name-error" class="error hidden">Name is required.</span>
  <button type="submit">Submit</button>
</form>


/* styles.css */
```

```
form {
  max-width: 400px;
  margin: 20px auto;
  padding: 20px;
  border: 1px solid #ccc;
  border-radius: 8px;
}
.error {
  color: red;
  font-size: 0.9rem;
}
.hidden {
  display: none;
}
button {
  background-color: var(--primary);
  color: white;
  padding: 10px;
}

// script.js
const form = document.getElementById('contact-form');
```

```
const nameInput = document.getElementById('name');
const nameError = document.getElementById('name-error');

form.addEventListener('submit', (e) => {
  e.preventDefault();
  if (nameInput.value.trim() === '') {
    nameError.classList.remove('hidden');
  } else {
    nameError.classList.add('hidden');
    alert(`Thank you, ${nameInput.value}!`);
  }
});
```

This form uses semantic HTML for structure, CSS for styling and error visibility, and JavaScript for validation and interactivity.

## Challenges and Solutions

- **Challenge**: JavaScript errors breaking functionality.

**Solution**: Use error handling (e.g., `try/catch`) and test thoroughly:

```
try {
  document.getElementById('missing').style.color = 'blue';
} catch (error) {
  console.error('Element not found:', error);
}
```

- **Challenge**: CSS overriding JavaScript-applied styles.

**Solution**: Ensure specificity or use `!important` sparingly:

```
.active {
  background-color: #007bff !important;
}
```

- **Challenge**: Inconsistent rendering across browsers.
  - **Solution**: Use a CSS reset and test with tools like BrowserStack.

## Tools for Integration

- **Linters**: ESLint for JavaScript, Stylelint for CSS, and HTMLHint for HTML ensure consistency.
- **Preprocessors**: Sass or Less enhance CSS with variables and mixins.
- **Build Tools**: Webpack or Vite bundle and optimize assets.
- **Browser DevTools**: Inspect HTML, CSS, and JavaScript in real-time.
- **Version Control**: Git tracks changes across files.

## Benefits of Effective Integration

- **Maintainability**: Separated files and modular code simplify updates.
- **Scalability**: Reusable styles and scripts support large projects.
- **User Experience**: Dynamic, responsive designs enhance engagement.
- **Accessibility**: Semantic HTML and ARIA attributes ensure inclusivity.
- **Performance**: Optimized integration reduces load times.

---

# 6.2 Planning and Designing a Multi-Page Website

## The Importance of Planning and Design

Planning and designing a multi-page website is a critical step in web development, ensuring a cohesive, user-friendly, and scalable product. A well-planned website aligns with user needs, business goals, and technical constraints, while a thoughtful design enhances usability, aesthetics, and accessibility. A multi-page website, with distinct pages for content like home, about, services, and contact, requires careful organization to maintain consistency and navigation ease. This section explores the process of planning and designing a multi-page website, covering user research, wireframing, design principles, and technical considerations.

## Step 1: Defining Goals and Audience

Before coding, define the website's purpose and target audience:

- **Goals**: Identify objectives, such as selling products, sharing information, or building a portfolio. For example, an e-commerce site aims to drive sales, while a blog focuses on content delivery.
- **Audience**: Understand user demographics, preferences, and needs. For instance, a portfolio site for freelancers targets potential clients, requiring professional design and clear calls-to-action.
- **User Stories**: Create scenarios like "As a visitor, I want to contact the owner easily" to guide design decisions.

## Step 2: Content Planning

Plan the content and structure for each page:

- **Site Map**: Outline the website's structure, e.g.:
    - Home (`index.html`): Overview and welcome.
    - About (`about.html`): Background and mission.
    - Services (`services.html`): Offerings or portfolio.
    - Contact (`contact.html`): Form and details.
- **Content Inventory**: List elements like text, images, forms, or videos. For example, the home page might include a hero image, headline, and navigation menu.

**Navigation**: Design a consistent navigation menu, using a <nav> element with links to all pages:

```
<nav>

  <ul>

    <li><a href="index.html">Home</a></li>

    <li><a href="about.html">About</a></li>

    <li><a href="services.html">Services</a></li>

    <li><a href="contact.html">Contact</a></li>

  </ul>

</nav>
```

- 

## Step 3: Wireframing and Prototyping

Wireframes and prototypes visualize the site's layout and functionality:

- **Wireframes**: Create low-fidelity sketches (using tools like Figma or Balsamiq) to map out page layouts. For example, the home page might have a header, hero section, content area, and footer.
- **Prototypes**: Build interactive mockups (e.g., in Figma or Adobe XD) to test navigation and user flow. Include placeholders for dynamic elements like forms or carousels.

**Responsive Design**: Plan layouts for desktop, tablet, and mobile using CSS media queries:

```
@media (max-width: 600px) {

  nav ul {

    flex-direction: column;

  }

}
```

•

## Step 4: Design Principles

Apply design principles to ensure usability and aesthetics:

**Consistency**: Use a unified color scheme, typography, and layout across pages. Define CSS variables:

```
:root {

  --primary: #007bff;

  --font: 'Roboto', sans-serif;

}

body {

  font-family: var(--font);

}
```

- 
- **Hierarchy**: Use headings, font sizes, and spacing to guide attention. For example, `<h1>` for page titles, `<h2>` for sections.
- **Accessibility**: Ensure semantic HTML, sufficient contrast (WCAG 4.5:1), and keyboard navigation.
- **Simplicity**: Avoid cluttered designs; prioritize clear content and intuitive navigation.
- **Visual Appeal**: Use images, icons, and whitespace to enhance aesthetics.

## Step 5: Technical Considerations

Plan the technical implementation:

**File Structure**: Organize files for scalability:

```
my-website/

├── css/

│   └── styles.css
```

```
├── js/
│   └── script.js
├── images/
├── index.html
├── about.html
├── services.html
├── contact.html
```

- 
- **Performance**: Optimize images (e.g., WebP format), minify CSS/JavaScript, and use lazy loading (`loading="lazy"`).

**SEO**: Include meta tags and semantic HTML:

```
<meta name="description" content="A professional portfolio website">
```

- 

**JavaScript Features**: Plan interactive elements, like form validation or dynamic content:

```
document.querySelector('form').addEventListener('submit', (e) => {

  e.preventDefault();

  alert('Form submitted!');

});
```

- 

## Step 6: Iterative Development and Testing

- **Build Incrementally**: Develop one page at a time, starting with the home page.
- **Test Continuously**: Use browser dev tools to check responsiveness, accessibility (with WAVE or Lighthouse), and cross-browser compatibility (with BrowserStack).

- **User Feedback**: Test with real users to refine navigation and design.

## Practical Example: Multi-Page Portfolio Site

Plan a portfolio site with four pages:

- **Home**: Hero section, featured work, and call-to-action.
- **About**: Bio, skills, and photo.
- **Services**: List of offerings.
- **Contact**: Form and social links.

**Sample Code (index.html)**:

```
<!DOCTYPE html>

<html lang="en">

<head>

    <meta charset="UTF-8">

    <meta name="viewport" content="width=device-width, initial-scale=1.0">

    <meta name="description" content="Professional portfolio">

    <title>My Portfolio</title>

    <link rel="stylesheet" href="css/styles.css">

</head>

<body>

    <header>

        <h1>My Portfolio</h1>

        <nav aria-label="Main navigation">

            <ul>

                <li><a href="index.html" aria-current="page">Home</a></li>
```

```
            <li><a href="about.html">About</a></li>
            <li><a href="services.html">Services</a></li>
            <li><a href="contact.html">Contact</a></li>
          </ul>
       </nav>
    </header>
    <main>
       <section class="hero">
          <h2>Welcome to My Work</h2>
          <p>Discover my projects and skills.</p>
          <button id="cta">Explore Now</button>
       </section>
    </main>
    <footer>
       <p>&copy; 2025 My Portfolio</p>
    </footer>
    <script src="js/script.js"></script>
</body>
</html>
```

**CSS (styles.css)**:

```
:root {
```

```
    --primary: #007bff;
}
body {
    font-family: 'Roboto', sans-serif;
    margin: 0;
}
header {
    background-color: var(--primary);
    color: white;
    text-align: center;
    padding: 20px;
}
nav ul {
    display: flex;
    justify-content: center;
    gap: 20px;
    list-style: none;
}
.hero {
    text-align: center;
    padding: 50px;
}
```

**JavaScript (script.js)**:

```
document.getElementById('cta').addEventListener('click', () => {

  alert('Explore my portfolio!');

});
```

### Challenges and Solutions

- **Challenge**: Inconsistent design across pages.
  - **Solution**: Use a shared CSS file and reusable components.
- **Challenge**: Poor navigation on mobile.
  - **Solution**: Implement a responsive menu with JavaScript toggle.
- **Challenge**: Slow load times.
  - **Solution**: Optimize images and minify assets.

## 6.3 Hands-On Project: Build a Portfolio Website

### Project Overview

This hands-on project guides you through building a multi-page portfolio website using HTML, CSS, and JavaScript, integrating the skills learned in previous chapters. The portfolio will showcase your work, skills, and contact information across four pages: Home, About, Projects, and Contact. The site will feature semantic HTML for structure, responsive CSS for styling, and JavaScript for interactivity, such as a theme toggle and form validation. This project reinforces best practices in web development, including accessibility, performance optimization, and modular design, preparing you to create a professional online presence.

### Step 1: Planning the Portfolio Website

Before coding, plan the site's structure, content, and functionality:

- **Goals**: Create a professional portfolio to showcase skills and projects, attract clients or employers, and demonstrate web development proficiency.

- **Pages**:
  - **Home**: Hero section with a welcome message, call-to-action, and featured project.
  - **About**: Personal bio, skills list, and profile image.
  - **Projects**: Gallery of project cards with descriptions and links.
  - **Contact**: Form for inquiries and social media links.
- **Features**:
  - Responsive navigation menu.
  - Theme toggle (light/dark mode) using JavaScript.
  - Contact form with client-side validation.
  - Accessible design with semantic HTML and ARIA attributes.
- **Content**: Gather text (e.g., bio, project descriptions), images (e.g., profile photo, project screenshots), and links to external projects or social profiles.

## Step 2: Setting Up the Project

Create a folder named `portfolio-website` with the following structure:

```
portfolio-website/
├── css/
│   └── styles.css
├── js/
│   └── script.js
├── images/
│   ├── profile.jpg
│   ├── project1.jpg
│   └── project2.jpg
├── index.html
├── about.html
├── projects.html
```

```
├── contact.html
```

- Download royalty-free images for `profile.jpg`, `project1.jpg`, and `project2.jpg` (e.g., from Unsplash).
- Use Visual Studio Code with Live Server for real-time previews.

## Step 3: Creating the HTML Structure

Each page will share a consistent layout with a header, navigation, main content, and footer. Below is the code for `index.html` (other pages will follow a similar structure):

```
<!-- index.html -->

<!DOCTYPE html>

<html lang="en">

<head>

  <meta charset="UTF-8">

  <meta name="viewport" content="width=device-width, initial-scale=1.0">

  <meta name="description" content="Personal portfolio showcasing web
development projects">

  <title>My Portfolio - Home</title>

  <link rel="stylesheet" href="css/styles.css">

</head>

<body>

  <header>

    <h1>My Portfolio</h1>

    <nav aria-label="Main navigation">
```

```
        <ul>
          <li><a href="index.html" aria-current="page">Home</a></li>
          <li><a href="about.html">About</a></li>
          <li><a href="projects.html">Projects</a></li>
          <li><a href="contact.html">Contact</a></li>
        </ul>
        <button id="theme-toggle" aria-label="Toggle dark mode"> </button>
      </nav>
    </header>
    <main>
      <section class="hero">
        <h2>Welcome to My Portfolio</h2>
        <p>I'm a web developer passionate about creating user-friendly websites.</p>
        <a href="projects.html" class="cta">View My Work</a>
      </section>
      <section class="featured">
        <h2>Featured Project</h2>
        <div class="project-card">
          <img src="images/project1.jpg" alt="Screenshot of project one" loading="lazy">
          <h3>Project One</h3>
          <p>A responsive web app built with HTML, CSS, and JavaScript.</p>
```

```
                <a href="https://example.com" target="_blank" rel="noopener">Live
Demo</a>
            </div>
        </section>
    </main>
    <footer>
        <p>&copy; 2025 My Portfolio. All rights reserved.</p>
    </footer>
    <script src="js/script.js"></script>
</body>
</html>
```

**About Page (about.html)**:

```
<!-- about.html -->
<!DOCTYPE html>
<html lang="en">
<head>
    <meta charset="UTF-8">
    <meta name="viewport" content="width=device-width, initial-scale=1.0">
    <meta name="description" content="About the web developer">
    <title>My Portfolio - About</title>
    <link rel="stylesheet" href="css/styles.css">
```

```
</head>

<body>

  <header>

    <h1>My Portfolio</h1>

    <nav aria-label="Main navigation">

      <ul>

        <li><a href="index.html">Home</a></li>

        <li><a href="about.html" aria-current="page">About</a></li>

        <li><a href="projects.html">Projects</a></li>

        <li><a href="contact.html">Contact</a></li>

      </ul>

      <button id="theme-toggle" aria-label="Toggle dark mode"> </button>

    </nav>

  </header>

  <main>

    <section class="about">

      <h2>About Me</h2>

      <img src="images/profile.jpg" alt="Profile photo" loading="lazy">

      <p>I'm a passionate web developer with expertise in HTML, CSS, and JavaScript.</p>

      <h3>Skills</h3>

      <ul>
```

```
            <li>Responsive Web Design</li>
            <li>JavaScript and DOM Manipulation</li>
            <li>Accessibility and SEO</li>
          </ul>
        </section>
    </main>
    <footer>
        <p>&copy; 2025 My Portfolio. All rights reserved.</p>
    </footer>
    <script src="js/script.js"></script>
</body>
</html>
```

**Projects Page (projects.html)**:

```
<!-- projects.html -->
<!DOCTYPE html>
<html lang="en">
<head>
    <meta charset="UTF-8">
    <meta name="viewport" content="width=device-width, initial-scale=1.0">
    <meta name="description" content="Portfolio projects">
    <title>My Portfolio - Projects</title>
```

```html
    <link rel="stylesheet" href="css/styles.css">
</head>
<body>
    <header>
        <h1>My Portfolio</h1>
        <nav aria-label="Main navigation">
            <ul>
                <li><a href="index.html">Home</a></li>
                <li><a href="about.html">About</a></li>
                <li><a href="projects.html" aria-current="page">Projects</a></li>
                <li><a href="contact.html">Contact</a></li>
            </ul>
            <button id="theme-toggle" aria-label="Toggle dark mode">🌙</button>
        </nav>
    </header>
    <main>
        <section class="projects">
            <h2>My Projects</h2>
            <div class="project-grid">
                <div class="project-card">
                    <img src="images/project1.jpg" alt="Screenshot of project one"
loading="lazy">
```

```
            <h3>Project One</h3>

            <p>A responsive web app.</p>

            <a href="https://example.com" target="_blank" rel="noopener">Live
Demo</a>

          </div>

          <div class="project-card">

            <img src="images/project2.jpg" alt="Screenshot of project two"
loading="lazy">

            <h3>Project Two</h3>

            <p>An interactive dashboard.</p>

            <a href="https://example.com" target="_blank" rel="noopener">Live
Demo</a>

          </div>

        </div>

      </section>

    </main>

    <footer>

      <p>&copy; 2025 My Portfolio. All rights reserved.</p>

    </footer>

    <script src="js/script.js"></script>

</body>

</html>
```

**Contact Page (contact.html)**:

```
<!-- contact.html -->

<!DOCTYPE html>

<html lang="en">

<head>

  <meta charset="UTF-8">

  <meta name="viewport" content="width=device-width, initial-scale=1.0">

  <meta name="description" content="Contact the web developer">

  <title>My Portfolio - Contact</title>

  <link rel="stylesheet" href="css/styles.css">

</head>

<body>

  <header>

    <h1>My Portfolio</h1>

    <nav aria-label="Main navigation">

      <ul>

        <li><a href="index.html">Home</a></li>

        <li><a href="about.html">About</a></li>

        <li><a href="projects.html">Projects</a></li>

        <li><a href="contact.html" aria-current="page">Contact</a></li>

      </ul>

      <button id="theme-toggle" aria-label="Toggle dark mode">🌙</button>
```

```
    </nav>

  </header>

  <main>

    <section class="contact">

      <h2>Contact Me</h2>

      <form id="contact-form">

        <div>

          <label for="name">Name:</label>

          <input id="name" type="text" required aria-required="true">

          <span id="name-error" class="error hidden">Name is required.</span>

        </div>

        <div>

          <label for="email">Email:</label>

          <input id="email" type="email" required aria-required="true">

          <span id="email-error" class="error hidden">Valid email is
required.</span>

        </div>

        <button type="submit">Send</button>

      </form>

      <p>Follow me on <a href="https://example.com" target="_blank"
rel="noopener">GitHub</a>.</p>

    </section>

  </main>
```

```
    <footer>
        <p>&copy; 2025 My Portfolio. All rights reserved.</p>
    </footer>
    <script src="js/script.js"></script>
</body>
</html>
```

### Step 4: Styling with CSS (`css/styles.css`)

In `styles.css`, add:

```
/* Reset and Box Model */
* {
    box-sizing: border-box;
    margin: 0;
    padding: 0;
}

/* Root Variables */
:root {
    --primary: #007bff;
    --background: #f4f4f4;
    --text: #333;
}
```

```
/* Body */
body {
    font-family: 'Roboto', Arial, sans-serif;
    background-color: var(--background);
    color: var(--text);
    line-height: 1.6;
}

body.dark {
    background-color: #333;
    color: #f4f4f4;
}

/* Header */
header {
    background-color: var(--primary);
    color: white;
    text-align: center;
    padding: 20px;
    margin-bottom: 20px;
}
```

```
header h1 {
    font-size: 2.5rem;
}

nav {
    display: flex;
    justify-content: space-between;
    align-items: center;
    padding: 10px;
}

nav ul {
    display: flex;
    gap: 20px;
    list-style: none;
}

nav a {
    color: white;
    text-decoration: none;
}
```

```
nav a:hover, nav a[aria-current="page"] {
    color: #e0e0e0;
}

#theme-toggle {
    background: none;
    border: none;
    font-size: 1.5rem;
    cursor: pointer;
}

/* Main */
main {
    max-width: 1000px;
    margin: 0 auto;
    padding: 20px;
}

.hero {
    text-align: center;
    padding: 50px 20px;
```

```
    background-color: white;
    border-radius: 8px;
}

.cta {
    display: inline-block;
    padding: 10px 20px;
    background-color: var(--primary);
    color: white;
    text-decoration: none;
    border-radius: 5px;
}

.cta:hover {
    background-color: #0056b3;
}

.project-grid {
    display: grid;
    grid-template-columns: repeat(auto-fit, minmax(300px, 1fr));
    gap: 20px;
}
```

```
.project-card {
    background-color: white;
    padding: 20px;
    border: 1px solid #ccc;
    border-radius: 8px;
    text-align: center;
}

.project-card img {
    max-width: 100%;
    height: auto;
    border-radius: 5px;
}

.about img {
    max-width: 200px;
    display: block;
    margin: 20px auto;
}

form {
```

```
    display: flex;
    flex-direction: column;
    gap: 15px;
    max-width: 400px;
    margin: 20px auto;
}

form div {
    display: flex;
    flex-direction: column;
}

input {
    padding: 10px;
    border: 1px solid #ccc;
    border-radius: 5px;
}

.error {
    color: red;
    font-size: 0.9rem;
}
```

```
.hidden {
    display: none;
}

button {
    padding: 10px;
    background-color: var(--primary);
    color: white;
    border: none;
    border-radius: 5px;
    cursor: pointer;
}

button:hover {
    background-color: #0056b3;
}

/* Footer */
footer {
    text-align: center;
    padding: 20px;
```

```
    color: #666;
}

/* Responsive Design */
@media (max-width: 600px) {
    nav ul {
        flex-direction: column;
        align-items: center;
    }
    .hero {
        padding: 30px 10px;
    }
}
```

## Step 5: Adding JavaScript (`js/script.js`)

In `script.js`, add:

```
// Theme Toggle
const toggleButton = document.getElementById('theme-toggle');
toggleButton.addEventListener('click', () => {
    document.body.classList.toggle('dark');
    toggleButton.textContent = document.body.classList.contains('dark') ? '☀️' : '🌙';
});
```

```
// Form Validation
const form = document.getElementById('contact-form');
if (form) {
  const nameInput = document.getElementById('name');
  const emailInput = document.getElementById('email');
  const nameError = document.getElementById('name-error');
  const emailError = document.getElementById('email-error');

  form.addEventListener('submit', (e) => {
    e.preventDefault();
    let valid = true;

    if (nameInput.value.trim() === '') {
      nameError.classList.remove('hidden');
      valid = false;
    } else {
      nameError.classList.add('hidden');
    }

    if (!emailInput.value.includes('@')) {
      emailError.classList.remove('hidden');
```

```
            valid = false;
        } else {
            emailError.classList.add('hidden');
        }

        if (valid) {
            alert(`Thank you, ${nameInput.value}! Your message has been sent.`);
            form.reset();
        }
    });
}
```

This JavaScript adds a dark mode toggle and validates the contact form, ensuring accessibility and interactivity.

## Step 6: Testing and Validation

- **Test Functionality**: Open `index.html` with Live Server to verify navigation, theme toggle, form validation, and image loading.
- **Check Responsiveness**: Use Chrome DevTools' device mode to test mobile layouts.
- **Validate Code**: Use W3C Markup Validator for HTML and CSS Validator for CSS.
- **Accessibility**: Test with WAVE or Lighthouse, ensuring keyboard navigation and ARIA attributes.
- **Cross-Browser Testing**: Verify in Chrome, Firefox, Safari, and Edge using BrowserStack.

## Step 7: Enhancements

- Add a project filter (e.g., by category) using JavaScript.
- Include a testimonial section with a carousel.
- Optimize images with WebP and lazy loading.
- Deploy to a hosting platform (see Section 6.4).

---

# 6.4 Deploying Your Website: Making It Live

## The Importance of Deployment

Deploying a website transforms your local project into a publicly accessible resource, allowing users worldwide to access it. Deployment involves hosting your site's files on a server, configuring a domain, and ensuring performance, security, and accessibility. This process is a critical step in web development, as it bridges the gap between development and real-world use. This section covers the deployment process, including choosing a hosting provider, configuring servers, optimizing for production, and maintaining a live website, ensuring your portfolio or project is available to a global audience.

## Understanding Web Hosting

Web hosting involves storing your website's files (HTML, CSS, JavaScript, images) on a server that's accessible via the internet. Key hosting types include:

- **Shared Hosting**: Multiple websites share a server (e.g., Bluehost, HostGator). Affordable but limited for high-traffic sites.
- **VPS Hosting**: Virtual private servers offer dedicated resources (e.g., DigitalOcean, Linode).
- **Cloud Hosting**: Scalable hosting on cloud platforms (e.g., AWS, Google Cloud, Azure).
- **Static Hosting**: Ideal for static sites like portfolios (e.g., Netlify, GitHub Pages, Vercel).

For a portfolio website, static hosting is often sufficient, as it's cost-effective and simple to set up.

## Step 1: Preparing Your Site for Deployment

Before deploying, optimize your site:

**Minify Assets**: Use tools like CSSNano and UglifyJS to reduce CSS and JavaScript file sizes:

```
npm install -g cssnano

cssnano styles.css > styles.min.css
```

- 

**Optimize Images**: Convert to WebP or compress with TinyPNG. Use `loading="lazy"` for images:

```
<img src="image.webp" alt="Description" loading="lazy">
```

- 
- **Validate Code**: Run W3C validators for HTML and CSS to ensure compliance.
- **Test Locally**: Use Live Server to verify functionality, responsiveness, and accessibility.
- **Remove Debugging Code**: Delete `console.log()` statements and unused scripts.

## Step 2: Choosing a Hosting Provider

For a portfolio, free or low-cost static hosting is ideal:

- **GitHub Pages**: Free hosting for static sites, integrated with Git.
- **Netlify**: User-friendly platform with continuous deployment from Git.
- **Vercel**: Similar to Netlify, with support for modern frameworks.
- **Firebase Hosting**: Google's static hosting with CDN support.

This project uses GitHub Pages for simplicity.

## Step 3: Deploying with GitHub Pages

1. **Create a GitHub Repository**:

Initialize a Git repository in your `portfolio-website` folder:

```
git init

git add .
```

git commit -m "Initial commit"

- 

Create a repository on GitHub (e.g., `my-portfolio`) and push your code:

git remote add origin https://github.com/username/my-portfolio.git

git push -u origin main

- 

2. **Enable GitHub Pages**:
   - Go to the repository's Settings on GitHub.
   - Under "Pages," select the `main` branch and `/ (root)` folder.
   - Save, and GitHub will provide a URL (e.g., `https://username.github.io/my-portfolio`).
3. **Test the Live Site**:
   - Visit the provided URL to ensure all pages, styles, and scripts load correctly.
   - Check links, images, and JavaScript functionality.

## Step 4: Configuring a Custom Domain (Optional)

To use a custom domain (e.g., `yourname.com`):

- Purchase a domain from a registrar like Namecheap or GoDaddy.
- In GitHub Pages settings, add the domain (e.g., `www.yourname.com`).
- Configure DNS settings with your registrar:
  - Add an `A` record pointing to GitHub's IP addresses (e.g., `185.199.108.153`).
  - Add a `CNAME` record for `www` pointing to `username.github.io`.

Update your repository with a `CNAME` file:

www.yourname.com

- 

## Step 5: Optimizing for Production

- **Enable HTTPS**: GitHub Pages and most hosting platforms provide free SSL certificates for secure connections.
- **Use a CDN**: Platforms like Netlify and Vercel automatically use Content Delivery Networks for faster load times.

**Set Cache Headers**: Configure long-term caching for static assets:

```
<FilesMatch "\.(css|js|jpg|png|webp)$">

  Header set Cache-Control "max-age=31536000, public"

</FilesMatch>
```

**SEO Optimization**: Add meta tags and a sitemap:

```
<meta name="description" content="My portfolio website">
```

Create a `sitemap.xml`:

```
<?xml version="1.0" encoding="UTF-8"?>

<urlset xmlns="http://www.sitemaps.org/schemas/sitemap/0.9">

  <url>

    <loc>https://yourname.com/</loc>

  </url>

  <url>

    <loc>https://yourname.com/about</loc>

  </url>

</urlset>
```

## Step 6: Maintaining the Live Site

- **Monitor Performance**: Use Google Analytics or Lighthouse to track load times and user behavior.

**Update Content**: Push changes to GitHub to update the live site:
git add .

git commit -m "Update project section"

git push

- 
- **Test Regularly**: Verify functionality, responsiveness, and accessibility after updates.
- **Backup**: Maintain a local copy and use version control to prevent data loss.

## Challenges and Solutions

- **Challenge**: Broken links or assets after deployment.
  - **Solution**: Use relative paths (e.g., `css/styles.css`) and test locally first.
- **Challenge**: Slow load times.
  - **Solution**: Optimize images, minify assets, and use a CDN.
- **Challenge**: Cross-browser issues.
  - **Solution**: Test with BrowserStack and include polyfills if needed.

## Practical Example

Deploy the portfolio from Section 6.3:

- Push the `portfolio-website` folder to a GitHub repository.
- Enable GitHub Pages and visit the generated URL.
- Verify the theme toggle, form validation, and responsive navigation.
- Add a custom domain if desired, following the steps above.

---

# 6.5 Next Steps: Exploring Advanced Web Development Topics

## The Path Forward in Web Development

Completing a portfolio website marks a significant milestone in your web development journey, but the field is vast and constantly evolving. Advanced topics build on your foundation in HTML, CSS, and JavaScript, enabling you to create more complex, scalable, and modern applications. Exploring frameworks, backend development, performance optimization, and emerging technologies prepares you for professional projects and career growth. This section outlines key advanced topics, learning strategies, and resources to guide your next steps in web development.

## Advanced Front-End Development

### 1. JavaScript Frameworks

Frameworks like React, Vue.js, and Angular streamline the development of dynamic, single-page applications (SPAs):

**React**: A library for building component-based UIs. Learn to create reusable components:

```
function Welcome() {

   return <h1>Hello, React!</h1>;

}
```

- 
- **Vue.js**: Lightweight and beginner-friendly, ideal for progressive enhancements.
- **Angular**: A full-fledged framework for enterprise applications.

**Next Steps**: Start with React via Create React App, follow tutorials on react.dev, and build a small SPA.

### 2. State Management

Manage complex application state:

- **Redux** (React): Centralizes state for predictable updates.
- **Vuex** (Vue): Simplifies state management in Vue apps.
- **Context API**: Built-in React state management.

**Next Steps**: Learn Redux with a to-do list app, focusing on actions, reducers, and stores.

### 3. TypeScript

TypeScript adds static typing to JavaScript, improving code reliability:

```
interface User {

  name: string;

  age: number;

}

const user: User = { name: "Alice", age: 25 };
```

**Next Steps**: Convert a JavaScript project to TypeScript, using the TypeScript Playground.

## Backend Development

To become a full-stack developer, learn server-side technologies:

- **Node.js**: Run JavaScript on the server, enabling backend logic.

**Express**: A Node.js framework for building APIs:

```
const express = require('express');

const app = express();

app.get('/api', (req, res) => res.json({ message: 'Hello!' }));

app.listen(3000);
```

-

- **Databases**: Learn SQL (e.g., PostgreSQL) for relational data or NoSQL (e.g., MongoDB) for flexible schemas.

**Next Steps**: Build a REST API with Express and connect it to a MongoDB database.

## Performance Optimization

Advanced performance techniques include:

**Code Splitting**: Load JavaScript lazily with Webpack or Vite:

```
import('module').then(module => module.default());
```

- 
- **Server-Side Rendering (SSR)**: Use Next.js (React) or Nuxt.js (Vue) for faster initial loads.
- **Web Vitals**: Optimize Core Web Vitals (LCP, FID, CLS) using Lighthouse.

**Next Steps**: Implement code splitting in your portfolio and audit with Lighthouse.

## Accessibility and Testing

- **Advanced Accessibility**: Dive deeper into WCAG, ARIA landmarks, and screen reader testing.

**Automated Testing**: Use Jest for unit tests and Cypress for end-to-end tests:

```
test('adds 1 + 2', () => {

  expect(1 + 2).toBe(3);

});
```

- 

**Next Steps**: Write tests for your portfolio's form validation and test with NVDA.

## Emerging Technologies

**Progressive Web Apps (PWAs)**: Create app-like experiences with service workers:

```
if ('serviceWorker' in navigator) {

  navigator.serviceWorker.register('/sw.js');
```

```
}
```

- 
- **Web3**: Explore decentralized apps using Ethereum and Web3.js.
- **WebAssembly**: Use for performance-critical tasks, like games.

**Next Steps**: Build a simple PWA version of your portfolio with Workbox.

## Learning Strategies

- **Build Projects**: Apply new skills to real projects, like a blog or e-commerce site.
- **Contribute to Open Source**: Join GitHub projects to gain experience and collaborate.
- **Follow Tutorials**: Use resources like freeCodeCamp, The Odin Project, or MDN Web Docs.
- **Join Communities**: Participate in forums like Stack Overflow or Discord's web dev communities.
- **Stay Updated**: Follow blogs (e.g., Smashing Magazine, CSS-Tricks) and conferences (e.g., JSConf).

## Resources

- **Documentation**: MDN Web Docs, react.dev, vuejs.org.
- **Courses**: freeCodeCamp, Codecademy, Coursera.
- **Tools**: VS Code, BrowserStack, Postman for API testing.
- **Books**: "Eloquent JavaScript" by Marijn Haverbeke, "You Don't Know JS" by Kyle Simpson.

## Practical Example

Convert your portfolio to a React SPA:

```
<!-- index.html -->

<!DOCTYPE html>

<html lang="en">

<head>
```

```
    <meta charset="UTF-8">
    <title>React Portfolio</title>
</head>
<body>
    <div id="root"></div>
    <script src="https://unpkg.com/react@18/umd/react.production.min.js"></script>
    <script
src="https://unpkg.com/react-dom@18/umd/react-dom.production.min.js"></script>
    <script src="js/app.js"></script>
</body>
</html>


// js/app.js
const { useState } = React;


function App() {
    const [theme, setTheme] = useState('light');
    const toggleTheme = () => setTheme(theme === 'light' ? 'dark' : 'light');


    return (
        <div className={theme}>
            <header>
```

```
        <h1>My Portfolio</h1>

        <button onClick={toggleTheme}>Toggle Theme</button>

      </header>

    </div>

  );

}


ReactDOM.render(<App />, document.getElementById('root'));
```

# Chapter 7

# Resources and Further Learning

## 7.1 Recommended Tools and Extensions for Developers

### The Importance of Tools in Web Development

Web development is a multifaceted discipline that requires a robust set of tools to streamline workflows, enhance productivity, and ensure high-quality output. From coding to debugging, testing, and deployment, the right tools can significantly improve efficiency, reduce errors, and support best practices such as accessibility and performance optimization. For developers, especially beginners, choosing the appropriate tools and extensions is critical for mastering HTML, CSS, JavaScript, and advanced frameworks. This section explores recommended tools and extensions across various categories—code editors, browser tools, version control, testing, and more—providing a comprehensive guide to building a developer's toolkit.

### Code Editors and IDEs

A code editor or Integrated Development Environment (IDE) is the cornerstone of a developer's workflow, offering features like syntax highlighting, autocompletion, and debugging. Here are the top recommendations:

- **Visual Studio Code (VS Code)**:
  VS Code, developed by Microsoft, is a lightweight, open-source editor with a vast ecosystem of extensions. It supports HTML, CSS, JavaScript, and virtually any programming language. Key features include IntelliSense (smart autocompletion), integrated Git, and a built-in terminal.
  **Why Use It?**: Its flexibility, performance, and community support make it ideal for beginners and professionals.
  **Recommended Extensions**:
    - **Prettier**: Auto-formats code for consistent styling.

  - **ESLint**: Identifies JavaScript errors and enforces coding standards.
  - **Live Server**: Launches a local server for real-time HTML/CSS previews.
  - **HTML CSS Support**: Enhances HTML/CSS autocompletion.
  - **Debugger for Chrome**: Enables JavaScript debugging within VS Code.
- **Sublime Text**:
  A fast, lightweight editor known for its speed and simplicity. It supports multiple cursors, split editing, and a distraction-free mode.
  **Why Use It?**: Ideal for quick edits and small projects, with a minimal learning curve.
  **Extensions**: Install Package Control to add plugins like Emmet for rapid HTML/CSS coding.

- **JetBrains WebStorm**:
  A powerful IDE tailored for web development, with advanced features like code refactoring, testing integration, and support for frameworks like React and Angular.
  **Why Use It?**: Best for large-scale projects, though it's paid (with a free trial).
  **Extensions**: Built-in tools for JavaScript, TypeScript, and Node.js.

**Best Practice**: Start with VS Code for its versatility and free extensions, adding WebStorm for complex projects as needed.

## Browser Developer Tools

Browser developer tools are essential for testing, debugging, and optimizing websites. Every major browser offers built-in tools:

- **Google Chrome DevTools**:
  The industry standard, offering an Elements panel for HTML/CSS inspection, a Console for JavaScript debugging, a Network panel for monitoring resource loading, and a Performance tab for analyzing rendering.
  **Why Use It?**: Comprehensive and user-friendly, with features like device emulation for responsive testing.
  **Extensions**:

  - **Web Developer**: Adds a toolbar with CSS, form, and accessibility tools.

    - **ColorZilla**: Picks colors from webpages for CSS design.
    - **Lighthouse**: Audits performance, SEO, and accessibility.
- **Firefox Developer Tools**:
  Similar to Chrome, with unique features like a CSS Grid inspector and enhanced accessibility checks.
  **Why Use It?**: Strong for debugging CSS layouts and testing accessibility.

- **Safari Web Inspector**:
  Essential for testing on Apple devices, with tools for inspecting iOS-specific rendering.
  **Why Use It?**: Necessary for ensuring compatibility with Safari and iOS browsers.

**Best Practice**: Use Chrome DevTools for general development and Firefox/Safari for cross-browser testing.

## Version Control Tools

Version control is critical for managing code changes and collaborating with teams:

**Git**:
The industry-standard version control system, used to track changes, create branches, and collaborate via platforms like GitHub, GitLab, or Bitbucket.
**Why Use It?**: Essential for any project, from solo to enterprise.
**Commands to Learn**:

```
git init

git add .

git commit -m "Initial commit"

git push origin main
```

- 
- **GitHub Desktop**:
  A graphical interface for Git, simplifying commits and branch management.
  **Why Use It?**: Beginner-friendly alternative to command-line Git.

- **VS Code Git Integration**:
  Built-in Git support for committing, pushing, and pulling directly from the editor.
  **Why Use It?**: Streamlines version control within your coding environment.

**Best Practice**: Learn Git basics and use GitHub for hosting repositories, integrating with VS Code for seamless workflows.

## Package Managers and Build Tools

Package managers and build tools manage dependencies and optimize assets:

**npm**:
Node Package Manager, bundled with Node.js, installs libraries like React or Express.
**Why Use It?**: Essential for JavaScript projects.
**Example**:

```
npm install react
```

- 
- **Yarn**:
  A faster alternative to npm with improved dependency management.
  **Why Use It?**: Useful for large projects with complex dependencies.

**Vite**:
A modern build tool for fast development and production bundling.
**Why Use It?**: Replaces Webpack for simpler, faster builds.
**Example**:

```
npm create vite@latest my-project
```

- 
- **Webpack**:
  A powerful bundler for JavaScript, CSS, and assets.
  **Why Use It?**: Suitable for complex applications requiring custom configurations.

**Best Practice**: Start with npm and Vite for simplicity, exploring Webpack for advanced projects.

## Testing and Debugging Tools

Testing and debugging ensure code quality and performance:

**ESLint**:
A linter for JavaScript, catching errors and enforcing style guides.
**Why Use It?**: Improves code consistency and reduces bugs.
**Setup in VS Code**:

```
npm install eslint --save-dev

npx eslint --init
```

- 

**Jest**:
A testing framework for unit and integration tests.
**Why Use It?**: Ideal for testing JavaScript functions and React components.
**Example**:

```
test('adds 1 + 2', () => {

  expect(1 + 2).toBe(3);

});
```

- 
- **Cypress**:
  An end-to-end testing tool for simulating user interactions.
  **Why Use It?**: Ensures features like forms and navigation work as expected.

- **BrowserStack**:
  A cloud platform for cross-browser testing on real devices and browsers.
  **Why Use It?**: Verifies compatibility across Chrome, Firefox, Safari, and Edge.

**Best Practice**: Use ESLint for code quality, Jest for unit tests, and BrowserStack for cross-browser testing.

## Design and Prototyping Tools

Design tools help plan layouts and visuals:

- **Figma**:
  A collaborative design tool for creating wireframes, mockups, and prototypes.
  **Why Use It?**: Ideal for planning responsive layouts and collaborating with designers.

- **Adobe XD**:
  Similar to Figma, with strong integration for Adobe users.
  **Why Use It?**: Useful for high-fidelity prototypes.

**Best Practice**: Use Figma to create wireframes before coding, ensuring alignment between design and development.

## Accessibility and Performance Tools

- **WAVE**:
  A browser extension for evaluating accessibility compliance.
  **Why Use It?**: Identifies WCAG violations and suggests fixes.

- **Lighthouse**:
  Built into Chrome DevTools, audits performance, SEO, and accessibility.
  **Why Use It?**: Provides actionable insights for optimization.

- **WebPageTest**:
  Analyzes page load times and performance metrics.
  **Why Use It?**: Helps optimize for Core Web Vitals (LCP, FID, CLS).

**Best Practice**: Run Lighthouse and WAVE regularly to ensure accessibility and performance.

## Additional Utilities

- **Postman**: Tests API endpoints, crucial for backend integration.
- **CodePen**: An online editor for experimenting with HTML, CSS, and JavaScript.

- **Can I Use**: Checks browser support for HTML, CSS, and JavaScript features.
- **TinyPNG**: Compresses images for faster load times.

---

# 7.2 Online Communities and Forums for Support

## The Value of Community in Web Development

Web development is a collaborative and rapidly evolving field, and online communities and forums provide invaluable support for developers at all levels. These platforms offer opportunities to ask questions, share knowledge, troubleshoot issues, and stay updated on industry trends. From beginners seeking guidance to experts contributing to open-source projects, online communities foster learning, networking, and professional growth. This section explores the most impactful online communities and forums, detailing their features, benefits, and best practices for engagement to help developers thrive.

## Why Join Online Communities?

- **Problem-Solving**: Get answers to specific coding issues, from syntax errors to complex bugs.
- **Learning Opportunities**: Access tutorials, code reviews, and discussions on new technologies.
- **Networking**: Connect with peers, mentors, and potential employers or collaborators.
- **Career Growth**: Gain insights into job opportunities, best practices, and industry trends.
- **Community Contribution**: Share knowledge, answer questions, or contribute to open-source projects.

## Top Online Communities and Forums

### 1. Stack Overflow

- **Overview**: Stack Overflow is the leading Q&A platform for developers, covering HTML, CSS, JavaScript, and more.
- **Features**:
    - Searchable database of millions of questions and answers.

    - Tagging system (e.g., [javascript], [css]) for targeted searches.
    - Reputation system rewarding quality contributions.
- **Why Join?**: Ideal for solving specific technical issues, with a vast archive of solutions.
- **How to Use**:
    - Search before asking to avoid duplicates.

Provide minimal reproducible examples when posting:

```
<button onclick="myFunction()">Click</button>

<script>

  function myFunction() {

    console.log("Clicked"); // Not working

  }

</script>
```

    -
    - Follow the code of conduct and provide clear, concise questions.
- **Best Practice**: Upvote helpful answers and accept solutions to your questions.

**2. Reddit**

- **Overview**: Subreddits like r/webdev, r/javascript, r/css, and r/learnprogramming offer vibrant communities for discussion and advice.
- **Features**:
    - Informal discussions on trends, tools, and career paths.
    - AMAs (Ask Me Anything) with industry experts.
    - Community-driven resources and tutorials.
- **Why Join?**: Great for general advice, career tips, and staying updated on web development trends.
- **How to Use**:
    - Join relevant subreddits and participate in threads.
    - Share projects for feedback (e.g., post your portfolio in r/webdev).
    - Avoid self-promotion unless allowed by subreddit rules.
- **Best Practice**: Engage respectfully and contribute to discussions to build connections.

**3. Dev.to**

- **Overview**: A blogging and community platform for developers, with articles, tutorials, and discussions on web development.
- **Features**:
    - User-generated content on topics like React, accessibility, and career advice.
    - Comment sections for engaging with authors.
    - Tags (e.g., #webdev, #javascript) for filtering content.
- **Why Join?**: Ideal for learning through articles and connecting with a supportive community.
- **How to Use**:
    - Write blog posts to share your projects or insights.
    - Comment on articles to ask questions or provide feedback.
    - Follow tags to curate your feed.
- **Best Practice**: Publish tutorials or project walkthroughs to establish credibility.

**4. Discord**

- **Overview**: Discord hosts numerous web development servers, such as The Odin Project, freeCodeCamp, and JavaScript communities.
- **Features**:
    - Real-time chat for instant support.
    - Dedicated channels for HTML, CSS, JavaScript, and frameworks.
    - Voice channels for study groups or live coding.
- **Why Join?**: Offers immediate, conversational support and networking.
- **How to Use**:
    - Join servers via invites from community websites or Reddit.
    - Participate in channels like #help or #projects.

Share code snippets using markdown:

````
```javascript

console.log("Hello, World!");
````

- **Best Practice**: Be active, respectful, and follow server rules.
````

5. **GitHub Discussions**

- **Overview**: GitHub Discussions, available in many open-source repositories, allows developers to ask questions, share ideas, and collaborate.
- **Features**:
    - Integrated with GitHub repositories for project-specific support.
    - Threaded discussions for detailed problem-solving.
    - Collaboration with maintainers and contributors.
- **Why Join?**: Perfect for open-source contributors and project-specific queries.
- **How to Use**:
    - Explore repositories like React or Vue.js and join their Discussions tab.
    - Ask questions or report issues with clear details and code.
    - Contribute by answering questions or submitting pull requests.
- **Best Practice**: Read the repository's contribution guidelines before posting.

## Additional Communities

- **freeCodeCamp Forum**: A beginner-friendly forum with tutorials and challenges.
- **CSS-Tricks Forums**: Focused on CSS, with articles and discussions.
- **Hashnode**: A blogging platform with a developer community.
- **Slack Communities**: Groups like Frontend Developers or Women Who Code offer professional networking.

## Best Practices for Community Engagement

- **Be Respectful**: Follow community guidelines and maintain a positive tone.

**Ask Quality Questions**: Provide context, code snippets, and what you've tried:

```
// Why does this not toggle the class?

document.getElementById('btn').addEventListener('click', () => {

  document.body.classList.toggle('dark');

});
```

- 
- **Contribute Back**: Answer questions, share resources, or write tutorials.
- **Stay Active**: Regularly participate to build relationships and stay updated.

- **Avoid Spam**: Don't over-promote personal projects unless permitted.

## Benefits of Community Involvement

- **Faster Learning**: Get quick answers to coding problems.
- **Career Opportunities**: Network with recruiters and peers.
- **Inspiration**: Discover new tools, frameworks, and project ideas.
- **Support**: Find encouragement during challenging learning phases.
- **Portfolio Building**: Collaborate on open-source projects to showcase skills.

## Practical Example

Asking a question on Stack Overflow:

1. Search for existing answers (e.g., "JavaScript toggle class not working").
2. If unanswered, post a question:
    - **Title**: "Why does my JavaScript class toggle not work?"

**Body**:

```
<button id="btn">Toggle</button>

<script>

  document.getElementById('btn').addEventListener('click', () => {

    document.body.classList.toggle('dark');

  });

</script>

<!-- CSS -->

<style>

  .dark { background-color: #333; }

</style>
```

    - "I expect the background to change, but nothing happens. I tried debugging with console.log, but no errors appear."
3. Tag with `[javascript]`, `[css]`, and `[html]`.

4. Engage with responses and accept the best answer.

### Challenges and Solutions

- **Challenge**: Overwhelming number of communities.
    - **Solution**: Focus on one or two (e.g., Stack Overflow and Discord) initially.
- **Challenge**: Fear of asking "dumb" questions.
    - **Solution**: Communities welcome beginners; frame questions clearly and show effort.
- **Challenge**: Finding relevant answers.
    - **Solution**: Use specific keywords and tags when searching.

## 7.3 Free Resources for Continued Learning

### The Value of Free Learning Resources

The field of web development is dynamic, with new tools, techniques, and best practices emerging regularly. Free resources play a crucial role in enabling developers, especially beginners, to acquire and refine skills without financial barriers. These resources—ranging from tutorials and documentation to interactive platforms and open-source projects—provide accessible pathways to mastering HTML, CSS, JavaScript, and advanced topics like frameworks and backend development. By leveraging high-quality free resources, developers can stay updated, build projects, and grow their expertise at their own pace. This section explores a comprehensive array of free resources, detailing their features, benefits, and strategies for effective use.

### Online Learning Platforms

Free online platforms offer structured courses, tutorials, and coding challenges tailored to web development:

- **freeCodeCamp**
    - **Overview**: A non-profit platform offering a comprehensive curriculum covering HTML, CSS, JavaScript, React, Node.js, and more. It includes interactive coding challenges, projects, and certifications.
    - **Features**:

        - Over 8,000 tutorials and challenges.
        - Hands-on projects like building a portfolio or calculator.
        - Community forums for support.
    - **Why Use It?**: Ideal for beginners and intermediates, with a project-based approach that builds real-world skills.
    - **How to Use**: Start with the Responsive Web Design certification, complete challenges, and build the five required projects to earn a certificate.
    - **Example**: Learn HTML by completing challenges like creating a survey form.
- **The Odin Project**
    - **Overview**: A free, open-source curriculum focusing on full-stack development with Ruby, JavaScript, and databases.
    - **Features**:
        - Structured paths for front-end and full-stack development.
        - Emphasis on building projects like a clone of Google's homepage.
        - Active Discord community.
    - **Why Use It?**: Combines theory with practical projects, ideal for self-learners aiming for a career in development.
    - **How to Use**: Follow the JavaScript path, completing assignments and joining the Discord for peer support.
- **Codecademy (Free Tier)**
    - **Overview**: Offers free interactive courses on HTML, CSS, JavaScript, and frameworks like React.
    - **Features**:
        - In-browser coding environment.
        - Guided lessons with immediate feedback.
        - Free access to basic courses.
    - **Why Use It?**: Beginner-friendly with a hands-on approach to learning syntax and concepts.
    - **How to Use**: Start with the free HTML & CSS course, then progress to JavaScript basics.

## Documentation and Reference Materials

Official documentation provides authoritative, up-to-date information:

- **MDN Web Docs**
    - **Overview**: Mozilla's comprehensive resource for HTML, CSS, JavaScript, and web APIs.
    - **Features**:
        - Detailed guides, tutorials, and reference materials.
        - Code examples and browser compatibility tables.
        - Topics like accessibility, DOM manipulation, and Web APIs.
    - **Why Use It?**: The go-to reference for accurate, beginner-to-advanced content.
    - **How to Use**: Search for specific topics (e.g., "CSS Flexbox") or follow tutorials like "Getting Started with the Web."

**Example**: Use MDN to understand the `fetch` API:

```
fetch('https://api.example.com/data')

  .then(response => response.json())

  .then(data => console.log(data));
```

- **W3Schools**
    - **Overview**: A beginner-friendly resource with tutorials and examples for HTML, CSS, JavaScript, and more.
    - **Features**:
        - Simple explanations with "Try It Yourself" editors.
        - Covers SQL, Python, and web frameworks.
        - Reference sections for tags and properties.
    - **Why Use It?**: Great for quick learning and experimenting with code.
    - **How to Use**: Practice CSS Grid by modifying examples in their online editor.

## Interactive Coding Platforms

Interactive platforms allow hands-on practice:

- **CodePen**
    - **Overview**: An online code editor for experimenting with HTML, CSS, and JavaScript.

- **Features**:
  - Real-time previews of code.
  - Community pens for inspiration.
  - Debugging and sharing capabilities.
- **Why Use It?**: Perfect for prototyping and learning through community examples.
- **How to Use**: Create a pen to test a CSS animation or JavaScript function.

- **JSFiddle**
  - **Overview**: Similar to CodePen, with a focus on JavaScript-heavy projects.
  - **Features**:
    - Supports external libraries like React or jQuery.
    - Collaborative editing for team debugging.
  - **Why Use It?**: Useful for testing small scripts or sharing bugs with communities.
  - **How to Use**: Debug a DOM manipulation issue by sharing a fiddle on Stack Overflow.
- **Glitch**
  - **Overview**: A platform for building and hosting web apps, with a focus on JavaScript and Node.js.
  - **Features**:
    - Live previews and remixing of projects.
    - Free hosting for small apps.
  - **Why Use It?**: Ideal for building and deploying small projects quickly.
  - **How to Use**: Remix a sample project to learn Node.js APIs.

## Video Tutorials and YouTube Channels

Video content provides visual and guided learning:

- **Traversy Media**
  - **Overview**: A YouTube channel by Brad Traversy, offering tutorials on HTML, CSS, JavaScript, React, and Node.js.
  - **Features**:
    - Project-based videos (e.g., building a portfolio).
    - Clear explanations for beginners and intermediates.

    - **Why Use It?**: Practical, hands-on tutorials for real-world projects.
    - **How to Use**: Follow the "Build a Portfolio Website" tutorial to reinforce Chapter 6 skills.
- **The Net Ninja**
    - **Overview**: A YouTube channel with series on JavaScript, React, Firebase, and more.
    - **Features**:
        - Short, digestible videos.
        - Covers modern frameworks and tools.
    - **Why Use It?**: Great for learning frameworks like Vue.js or Svelte.
    - **How to Use**: Watch the JavaScript series to deepen DOM manipulation skills.
- **freeCodeCamp YouTube**
    - **Overview**: Offers long-form tutorials, crash courses, and coding bootcamps.
    - **Features**:
        - Covers full-stack development, APIs, and DevOps.
        - Free certifications.
    - **Why Use It?**: Comprehensive content for self-paced learning.
    - **How to Use**: Watch the "Full JavaScript Course" for a deep dive into ES6+ features.

## Open-Source Projects

Contributing to open-source projects builds practical experience:

- **GitHub**
    - **Overview**: Hosts thousands of open-source repositories for web development.
    - **Features**:
        - Issues labeled "good first issue" for beginners.
        - Collaboration with global developers.
    - **Why Use It?**: Enhances your portfolio and networking.
    - **How to Use**: Find beginner-friendly projects (e.g., freeCodeCamp's repository) and submit pull requests.
- **CodeTriage**

- **Overview**: A platform connecting developers with open-source issues.
- **Features**:
  - Curates issues by skill level and language.
  - Email notifications for new issues.
- **Why Use It?**: Simplifies finding contribution opportunities.
- **How to Use**: Sign up and filter for JavaScript projects.

## Blogs and Articles

Written content provides in-depth insights:

- **Smashing Magazine**
  - **Overview**: A web design and development blog with articles on accessibility, CSS, and JavaScript.
  - **Features**:
    - Expert-authored tutorials.
    - Covers UX, performance, and best practices.
  - **Why Use It?**: Offers advanced insights for professional development.
  - **How to Use**: Read articles on responsive design to enhance your portfolio.
- **CSS-Tricks**
  - **Overview**: A blog focused on CSS, with JavaScript and HTML content.
  - **Features**:
    - Practical guides (e.g., Flexbox vs. Grid).
    - Community comments for discussion.
  - **Why Use It?**: Great for mastering CSS layouts and techniques.
  - **How to Use**: Follow the Flexbox guide to improve your portfolio's layout.

## Strategies for Effective Learning

- **Set Goals**: Focus on specific skills (e.g., learn JavaScript arrays in a week).
- **Build Projects**: Apply knowledge by creating apps, like a to-do list or quiz (Chapter 4).
- **Practice Daily**: Use platforms like CodePen for quick coding exercises.

- **Combine Resources**: Pair video tutorials with documentation for deeper understanding.
- **Track Progress**: Maintain a GitHub repository to document projects and contributions.

### Challenges and Solutions

- **Challenge**: Overwhelm from too many resources.
    - **Solution**: Start with freeCodeCamp or The Odin Project for structure, then explore MDN for references.
- **Challenge**: Difficulty retaining concepts.
    - **Solution**: Build projects and revisit tutorials to reinforce learning.
- **Challenge**: Keeping up with updates.
    - **Solution**: Follow blogs like Smashing Magazine for industry trends.

---

## 7.4 Exploring Frameworks and Libraries

### The Role of Frameworks and Libraries

Frameworks and libraries are essential tools in modern web development, simplifying the creation of complex, scalable, and interactive applications. While HTML, CSS, and JavaScript provide the foundation, frameworks and libraries offer pre-built solutions, reusable components, and structured workflows to streamline development. Frameworks provide a full architecture for building applications, while libraries offer specific functionality. Exploring these tools expands your capabilities, enabling you to build professional-grade websites and applications efficiently. This section covers popular frameworks and libraries, their use cases, benefits, and strategies for learning them.

### Understanding Frameworks vs. Libraries

- **Frameworks**: Provide a structured environment with predefined rules and tools (e.g., React, Angular, Vue.js). They dictate the application's architecture, offering components, routing, and state management.
- **Libraries**: Offer specific tools or functions that you can integrate into your code (e.g., jQuery, Lodash). They provide flexibility but require manual integration.

## Popular Front-End Frameworks

### 1. React

- **Overview**: A JavaScript library (often called a framework) for building component-based user interfaces, developed by Facebook.
- **Features**:
  - Component-based architecture (e.g., `<Header />`, `<Footer />`).
  - Virtual DOM for efficient updates.
  - Ecosystem with tools like React Router and Redux.
- **Why Use It?**: Ideal for single-page applications (SPAs) like dashboards or social media platforms.

**Example**:

```
import React, { useState } from 'react';

function Counter() {

  const [count, setCount] = useState(0);

  return (

    <div>

      <p>Count: {count}</p>

      <button onClick={() => setCount(count + 1)}>Increment</button>

    </div>

  );

}
```

- 
- **Learning Path**: Start with the React documentation (react.dev), use Create React App, and build a to-do list app.

### 2. Vue.js

- **Overview**: A progressive framework for building UIs, known for its simplicity and flexibility.

- **Features**:
  - Reactive data binding.
  - Component-based structure.
  - Lightweight and beginner-friendly.
- **Why Use It?**: Great for small to medium projects or incremental adoption in existing sites.

**Example**:

```
const app = Vue.createApp({

  data() {

    return { message: 'Hello, Vue!' };

  }

});

app.mount('#app');
```

- 
- **Learning Path**: Follow Vue's official guide (vuejs.org) and build a small app using Vue CLI.

### 3. Angular

- **Overview**: A full-fledged framework by Google for enterprise-level applications.
- **Features**:
  - Two-way data binding.
  - Built-in tools for routing, forms, and testing.
  - Uses TypeScript for type safety.
- **Why Use It?**: Suitable for large, complex applications like CRMs.
- **Learning Path**: Start with Angular's official tutorial (angular.dev) and learn TypeScript basics.

## Popular Libraries

### 1. jQuery

- **Overview**: A lightweight library for DOM manipulation and AJAX.
- **Features**:

  - Simplifies event handling and animations.
  - Cross-browser compatibility.
- **Why Use It?**: Useful for legacy projects or quick DOM manipulation.

**Example**:
```
$('#myButton').on('click', () => {

  $('#myDiv').toggle();

});
```

- 
- **Learning Path**: Use jQuery's documentation (jquery.com) for small projects, but prioritize modern frameworks for new work.

**2. Lodash**

- **Overview**: A utility library for common JavaScript tasks (e.g., array manipulation, object handling).
- **Features**:
  - Functions like `_.map()`, `_.filter()`, and `_.debounce()`.
- **Why Use It?**: Enhances productivity for complex data operations.

**Example**:
```
const numbers = [1, 2, 3];

const doubled = _.map(numbers, n => n * 2); // [2, 4, 6]
```

- 
- **Learning Path**: Explore Lodash's documentation (lodash.com) and integrate into a project.

**3. GSAP (GreenSock Animation Platform)**

- **Overview**: A library for high-performance animations.
- **Features**:
  - Animates DOM elements, CSS properties, and SVGs.
  - Smooth, cross-browser animations.
- **Why Use It?**: Ideal for interactive UI effects.

**Example**:
```
gsap.to('.box', { x: 100, duration: 1 });
```

- 
- **Learning Path**: Follow GSAP's getting started guide (greensock.com) and animate a portfolio element.

## CSS Frameworks

- **Bootstrap**: A popular framework for responsive layouts and components.
    - **Why Use It?**: Quick prototyping with pre-built styles.

**Example**:
<button class="btn btn-primary">Click Me</button>

- 
    - 
    - **Learning Path**: Use Bootstrap's documentation (getbootstrap.com) to style a form.
- **Tailwind CSS**: A utility-first framework for custom designs.
    - **Why Use It?**: Flexible, modern approach to styling.

**Example**:
<div class="bg-blue-500 text-white p-4">Content</div>

- 
    - 
    - **Learning Path**: Follow Tailwind's guide (tailwindcss.com) to refactor your portfolio.

## Learning Strategies

- **Choose One Framework**: Start with React or Vue.js for front-end development.
- **Build Projects**: Create a blog, to-do app, or portfolio using a framework.
- **Use Official Docs**: Rely on react.dev, vuejs.org, or angular.dev for accurate guidance.
- **Join Communities**: Ask questions on Stack Overflow or Discord about framework-specific issues.
- **Experiment with Libraries**: Integrate Lodash or GSAP into small projects to understand their utility.

## Challenges and Solutions

- **Challenge**: Steep learning curve for frameworks.
  - **Solution**: Start with tutorials and small projects, focusing on one framework.
- **Challenge**: Choosing between frameworks.
  - **Solution**: Pick based on project needs (React for SPAs, Vue for simplicity, Angular for enterprise).
- **Challenge**: Keeping up with updates.
  - **Solution**: Follow framework blogs and changelogs.

---

# 7.5 Building Your Career as a Web Developer

## The Path to a Web Development Career

Web development offers a rewarding career with high demand, diverse opportunities, and the potential for creative and technical growth. As a web developer, you can work as a front-end, back-end, or full-stack developer, in roles ranging from freelance to corporate positions at tech giants. Building a successful career requires technical proficiency, a strong portfolio, networking, and continuous learning. This section outlines strategies for entering the field, advancing your skills, and thriving as a professional web developer, providing actionable steps to achieve career success.

## Steps to Start a Web Development Career

### 1. Build a Strong Foundation

Master core technologies:

- **HTML, CSS, JavaScript**: Complete projects like the portfolio in Chapter 6.
- **Frameworks**: Learn React or Vue.js for front-end roles.
- **Backend Basics**: Explore Node.js and Express for full-stack opportunities.

**Action**: Use freeCodeCamp or The Odin Project to solidify your skills.

### 2. Create a Portfolio

A portfolio showcases your skills to employers or clients:

- Include projects like the portfolio website, quiz app, or a blog.

- Host on GitHub Pages or Netlify.
- Highlight skills like responsive design, accessibility, and JavaScript interactivity.

**Action**: Build 3-5 diverse projects and deploy them online.

### 3. Gain Practical Experience

- **Freelancing**: Take small projects on platforms like Upwork or Fiverr.
- **Open Source**: Contribute to GitHub projects to gain experience and visibility.
- **Internships**: Apply for internships at startups or tech companies.

**Action**: Contribute to a beginner-friendly open-source project via CodeTriage.

### 4. Learn Job-Specific Skills

Tailor your skills to job roles:

- **Front-End**: Master React, CSS frameworks, and accessibility.
- **Back-End**: Learn Node.js, databases (MongoDB, PostgreSQL), and APIs.
- **Full-Stack**: Combine front-end and back-end skills with DevOps basics (e.g., Docker).

**Action**: Research job postings on LinkedIn to identify required skills.

## Networking and Professional Presence

- **LinkedIn**: Create a professional profile, share projects, and connect with recruiters.
- **GitHub**: Maintain an active profile with well-documented repositories.
- **Communities**: Join Stack Overflow, Reddit (r/webdev), and Discord for networking.
- **Conferences**: Attend virtual or in-person events like JSConf or React Conf.

**Action**: Post your portfolio on LinkedIn and engage in one community weekly.

## Job Search Strategies

- **Resume and Cover Letter**: Highlight technical skills, projects, and certifications.
- **Job Boards**: Apply on Indeed, Glassdoor, or We Work Remotely.

- **Portfolio Website**: Use your portfolio as a resume showcase.
- **Interviews**: Prepare for technical interviews with coding challenges on LeetCode or HackerRank.

**Action**: Practice common interview questions like "Explain the CSS box model."

## Continuous Learning

- **Stay Updated**: Follow blogs (Smashing Magazine, CSS-Tricks) and podcasts (Syntax, The Changelog).
- **Learn Advanced Topics**: Explore TypeScript, WebAssembly, or PWAs.
- **Certifications**: Consider free certifications from freeCodeCamp or paid ones like AWS Certified Developer.

**Action**: Dedicate 1-2 hours weekly to learning a new skill, like TypeScript.

## Freelancing vs. Full-Time Roles

- **Freelancing**: Offers flexibility but requires self-marketing and client management. Use platforms like Upwork or Freelancer.
- **Full-Time**: Provides stability and benefits. Target tech companies or startups.

**Action**: Try freelancing a small project to test the waters.

## Challenges and Solutions

- **Challenge**: Impostor syndrome.
    - **Solution**: Focus on completed projects and seek community support.
- **Challenge**: Competitive job market.
    - **Solution**: Build a unique portfolio and network actively.
- **Challenge**: Keeping skills current.
    - **Solution**: Follow industry trends and update your portfolio regularly.

## Practical Example

Update your portfolio with a job application focus:

- Add a resume page (`resume.html`) with skills, projects, and experience.
- Include a downloadable PDF resume using LaTeX (see below).
- Share the portfolio on LinkedIn and r/webdev.

**LaTeX Resume Example**:

```
\documentclass[a4paper,10pt]{article}

\usepackage[utf8]{inputenc}

\usepackage[T1]{fontenc}

\usepackage{geometry}

\geometry{margin=1in}


\begin{document}


\section*{John Doe}

\textbf{Web Developer} | john.doe@example.com | github.com/johndoe


\section*{Skills}

\begin{itemize}

  \item HTML, CSS, JavaScript, React

  \item Responsive Design, Accessibility

\end{itemize}


\section*{Projects}

\textbf{Portfolio Website} --- Built a multi-page site with HTML, CSS, and JavaScript.
Deployed on GitHub Pages.
```

```
\section*{Experience}

\textbf{Freelance Developer} | 2024--Present

\begin{itemize}

    \item Developed client websites using modern web technologies.

\end{itemize}


\end{document}
```

## Conclusion

Building a career as a web developer requires a blend of technical skills, a strong portfolio, networking, and continuous learning. By mastering core technologies, contributing to projects, and engaging with communities, you can secure freelance or full-time roles. Staying updated with industry trends and showcasing your work positions you for success in this dynamic, rewarding field.

# About the Book

"Web Development Unleashed: Master HTML, CSS, and JavaScript to Build Stunning, Interactive Websites" is your ultimate guide to mastering web development. This comprehensive book transforms beginners into confident developers by delivering hands-on, actionable strategies for creating professional websites. From crafting semantic HTML to designing responsive layouts with CSS and adding interactivity with JavaScript, you'll build real-world projects like a portfolio and quiz app. Packed with expert tips, debugging techniques, and deployment strategies, this book empowers you to create stunning, user-friendly websites that stand out. Start your journey to becoming a skilled web developer today!

# Book Description

Struggling to build websites that captivate users and showcase your skills? Frustrated by complex coding tutorials that leave you stuck? You're not alone—web development can feel overwhelming without clear, actionable guidance. Enter *Web Development Unleashed: Master HTML, CSS, and JavaScript to Build Stunning, Interactive Websites.* This isn't just another passive guide; it's a dynamic, results-driven roadmap to mastering web development. Whether you're a beginner or seeking to level up, this book delivers practical, step-by-step techniques to create stunning, interactive websites that engage and convert. Unlock the power of HTML, CSS, and JavaScript to build professional-grade sites and launch your career.

Discover how to:

- Create semantic HTML structures for accessible, SEO-friendly websites.
- Design responsive, visually appealing layouts using CSS Flexbox and Grid.
- Add dynamic interactivity with JavaScript, from form validation to real-time updates.
- Debug code efficiently and deploy stunning websites with confidence.
- Build real-world projects like portfolios and quiz apps to showcase your skills.

*Web Development Unleashed* cuts through the noise, offering clear, hands-on solutions to transform your ideas into reality. You'll gain the skills to craft user-friendly, interactive websites that stand out in today's digital landscape. Perfect for aspiring developers, freelancers, or anyone eager to master web development, this book empowers you to code with confidence and build a portfolio that opens doors. Don't let coding challenges hold you back—grab *Web Development Unleashed* now and start building stunning websites that make an impact.

www.ingramcontent.com/pod-product-compliance
Lightning Source LLC
LaVergne TN
LVHW060033210926
848481LV00013B/3852